Recovering the Past

THE

A HISTORIAN'S MEMOIR

Forrest McDonald

University Press of Kansas

© 2004 by the University Press of Kansas
All rights reserved
Published by the University Press of Kansas (Lawrence, Kansas 66049), which was
organized by the Kansas Board of Regents and is operated and funded by Emporia
State University, Fort Hays State University, Kansas State University, Pittsburg State
University, the University of Kansas, and Wichita State University.

Library of Congress Cataloging-in-Publication Data

McDonald, Forrest.
  Recovering the past : a historian's memoir / Forrest McDonald.
    p. cm.
  Includes bibliographical references (p.) and index.
  ISBN 0-7006-1329-3 (cloth : alk. paper)
    1. McDonald, Forrest. 2. Historians—United States—Biography.
3. Historiography—United States—History—20th century. 4. United States—
Historiography. I. Title.

E175.5.M395A3 2004
973'.072'02—dc22   2003069053

British Library Cataloguing-in-Publication Data is available.
Printed in the United States of America

10 9 8 7 6 5 4 3 2 1

Contents

Preface v

1: On the Historical Enterprise 1

2: The World as I Entered It 20

3: A New Game and a New Player 47

4: The Adventures of *We the People* 68

5: A Barefoot Boy in the Ivy League, and
a Lot of New Players 90

6: The Sixties, Seventies, and a Bit Beyond 113

7: The Grand (?) Finale 140

Appendix: The Intellectual World of
the Founding Fathers 167

Index 187

Preface

When one has spent more than half a century as a practicing historian, as I have, and if the experience has been rewarding, as mine has been, the compulsion to write about it becomes powerful, and a goodly number of historians have succumbed. Some choose to write mainly about historiography—meaning both the philosophy of history and the history of historical writing—and some opt for a form of autobiography. Still others essay an amalgam.

I have felt the urge for a time now, but I hesitated to undertake such a book. Almost everyone I know who has written one did it as a swan song, but I am not ready to put away my pen and write history no more. Therefore I deferred starting this book until I knew precisely what I wanted to write next. About a year ago the subject of the next book occurred to me, and as soon as this goes to press I shall begin work on it.

Having made the decision to go through with the project, I faced the question, to whom should the book be addressed? The norm is to write for fellow historians, but that seems to me to be wrong-headed and to result in stultifying reading. I have chosen, instead, to write for that elusive critter called the general reader, or, more precisely, for the vast number of people who genuinely love history for its own sake—which, as will become evident, I regard as eliminating a sizable majority of professional historians.

The last remark requires elaboration. During the middle decades of the nineteenth century, the era of such towering figures as George Bancroft, American historians wrote in broad, sweeping strokes and addressed their attention to the grand question of how the United States came to be what it was. They shared a naive faith in their discipline as a science and assumed that someday the full and absolute truth about the past would be known. They also shared a not-at-all naive belief that the United States was a thrice-blessed land and a beacon unto humankind. I happen to accept the latter bias without reservation: for all its faults, this country has more to be proud of and less to be ashamed of than any other nation on the face of the globe. I did not set out to prove that proposition; my instincts and my research led me to it, and I have little patience for those who say otherwise.

Toward the end of the nineteenth century and throughout the twentieth, the writing of history in America became the almost exclusive domain of academicians, with unforeseen consequences. Academic historians wrote monographs on esoteric and insufferably dull subjects not for an interested public but for an elite of eggheads. They came increasingly to believe that historians must justify their existence by pointing their research and writing toward the furtherance of a present public-policy agenda that they regard as desirable, and to insist that historians can behave in no other way. That conviction led them to view the past in terms of struggles between good people, whose goals squared with what they regarded as desirable, and bad people, whose goals did not.

Being constitutionally unable to share these assumptions—I study history because it gives me pleasure, and I do not care whether my writing has implications for current policy—I have from the beginning had a somewhat adversarial relationship with my chosen profession. Accordingly, I have found it necessary in composing this book to combine historiographical material with the autobiographical in order to place my work in context.

One more thing. This is a serious work, deadly serious, but I have tried to make it fun. I indicate in the first chapter that I think the main—and the purest—reason for studying history is that one finds it pleasurable. Thus if you enjoy the book, I do not apologize.

I am indebted to George Rable, Lawrence Kohl, Lance Banning, and Eugene Genovese for reading the manuscript and for making keen critical suggestions.

ONE

■

On the Historical Enterprise

To think historically is to organize memory along an abstracted concept of linear time. Such has been the prevailing mode of thought among Westerners since the eighteenth century, and so pervasive has it become that most Westerners, if they think about it at all, think it is "natural" to humankind. Rather than being natural, however, it is a learned, acquired, habitual way of remembering, one that could, despite its advantages, become outmoded or be displaced and abandoned.

The objects of historical thinking are varied, and people are often ambiguous as to what they mean by the term *history*. Always it refers to events that took place in the past, but never to all events. The evolution of the animal kingdom, changes in climate, and the alterations of the surface of the earth, for example, took place in the past and constitute what is sometimes called natural history, but these are outside the purview of conventional history, whose content is human affairs.[1] Nor does history encompass everything that has

---

1. The new field of environmental history has not yet shown that it is history rather than reinvigorated natural history, geology, paleontology, or expanded archaeology.

happened among humans, for prehistoric times are not included, by which term is meant times that predate existing records. Records comprise more than writings, for a shard, a vase, cave paintings, arrowheads, the ruins of monuments, preserved DNA, and diverse relics are clues to past human activity, but written documents, broadly defined, together with oral traditions, make up by far the greatest part of what is known and knowable about the past. Known and knowable are the key concepts: history is the remembered past, as perpetuated by words or by remnants of the past.

But the matter is more complex. Every society has a remembered past, commonly in the form of myths and legends about origins that are preserved by historians or by bards, poets, and storytellers. In an important sense, truth is irrelevant: so long as myths are generally accepted as true, they fulfill their function of legitimizing the society and its rules, rituals, symbols, and taboos, thereby making it viable. In another sense, truth or an approximation of it is crucial, for the operative myths can be undermined in myriad ways.

It is said that the ancient Greeks, specifically Herodotus, writing in the fifth century B.C., invented history by distinguishing what could be proved to have happened from what could not be so proved. The Greek word *historia*, which Herodotus used to describe his work, means to inquire into. The Roman statesman Cicero called Herodotus "the father of history," and Herodotus' work was truly innovative; but the credit must be tempered because only one other Greek of the century, Thucydides, followed Herodotus' example, after which the practice was substantially abandoned as being alien to Greek modes of thought. Far more in keeping with what would later be regarded as sound historical writing were the works of Polybius (second century B.C.), Caesar (d. 44 B.C.), Livy (d. A.D. 17), Plutarch (A.D. 46–119), and Tacitus (d. A.D. 120).[2]

2. Thomas Jefferson, in a letter to Anne Cory Bankhead dated December 8, 1808, described Tacitus as "the first writer in the world without a single exception. His book is a compound of history and morality of which we have no other example." See Carl

Neither the Greeks nor the Romans could go the whole distance toward a fully rounded conception of history, for though they had well-developed calendars, they had no means of reckoning time on a consecutively numbered linear scale. Most ancients, like most people throughout the ages, thought in terms of days and seasons and stages of life. The educated could locate events in time by referring to the period of the Gracchi or the reign of Augustus, but that was hardly satisfactory. Not until the seventh century did Isidore of Seville invent the system of dating forward and backward from the birth of Christ, thus establishing a universal (meaning throughout Christendom) chronological framework for events.[3]

The breakout to a modern historical mode of thinking began during the seventeenth century, with the rationalism of René Descartes and like-minded thinkers and especially with the publication of Sir Isaac Newton's *Principia Mathematica*. Using mathematical equations, Newton built upon Galileo's laws of ordinary motion to demonstrate that the movements of the planets, the sun, and the earth were governed by fixed and immutable laws. Newton himself was a devoutly religious man who fiercely rejected the rationalism of Descartes, but as his work came to be understood by increasing numbers of people, it progressively became fashionable to think of God as the infinitely perfect clock maker, who had set the universe in motion to be governed by invariable laws, then stepped back and let the laws operate. And if inanimate objects were governed by laws, the same must be true of humans: man needed merely to discover those laws to make a veritable heaven on earth possible.

Inane as that conceit was, it stimulated a flurry of historical research and writing throughout the eighteenth century. Until Edward Gibbon published his *Decline and Fall of the Roman Empire,* the

---

J. Richard, *The Founders and the Classics: Greece, Rome, and the American Enlightenment* (Cambridge, Mass., 1994), 54, and throughout for more restrained appraisals.

3. R. G. Collingwood, *The Idea of History* (Oxford, 1946), 51.

most widely read historians were Voltaire and David Hume. They developed fairly sophisticated techniques for evaluating historical documents, and they wrote brilliant narratives. Their work was marred by a contemptuous attitude toward history before the Reformation and particularly before the scientific revolution, based upon their hostility toward organized religion, as well as by a conviction that human nature was fixed and unalterable. "I believe," Hume could write at midcentury, "this to be the historical age and this the historical nation"; but he could also write that "the same motives always produce the same actions, the same events follow from the same causes." Partly because of its novelty and partly for philosophical reasons, history was suspect among scientists and philosophers. "We must consider how very little history there is," said Samuel Johnson, "I mean real authentic history. . . . all the colouring, all the philosophy of history is conjecture."[4]

The skepticism faded during the nineteenth century, when the Western world was swept by a euphoric belief in the inevitability of progress, and history appeared as the best measure of that progress. "Scientific history" flourished, starting with the German universities and spreading to the entire Western world. The Germans differed among themselves as to the mechanisms by which progress came about, but they agreed that the process unfolded historically, and they agreed that through diligent study the secrets of history would be unlocked. Scholars would pore over the records, sifting fact after fact and placing them side by side like grains of sand until they became a mountain. Then "the facts would speak for themselves." Each generation would improve upon the work of the last—that was inherent in the gospel of progress—but ultimately historians would reconstruct the past, in the words of Leopold von Ranke, *"wie es eigentlich gewesen,"* as it really happened.[5]

4. John Lukacs, *Historical Consciousness or the Remembered Past* (New York, 1968), 16–17.
5. Ibid., 40.

And that is where the Germans went wrong. History is a mode of thinking that wrenches the past out of context and sequence, out of the way it really happened, and reorders it in an artificial way that facilitates understanding and remembering.

This counterintuitive proposition can best be clarified by examples. The great historian and historiographical analyst J. H. Hexter has used the game of baseball to illustrate his conception of "historical tempo" as opposed to strict clock and calendar time. He asks the question, "Why did the New York baseball team win the National League pennant race in 1951?" He shows that a game-by-game analysis of the season would bore the reader to distraction and yield an unsatisfactory answer. His narrative answer begins not on opening day in April but with an account of the state of things on August 11, two-thirds of the way through the season, when the New York Giants were so far behind the league-leading Brooklyn Dodgers that sportswriters were counting them out. The next day, New York began a sixteen-game winning streak, which Hexter summarizes quickly. From there to the last scheduled games, Hexter's sense of historical tempo tells him to shun a chronicle of the remainder of the season as it really happened and to telescope groups of games until the season ended in a tie between New York and Brooklyn. Hexter then tells us, briefly, that in the ensuing best-of-three playoff series, the teams split the first two games. In the decisive final game, he summarizes the scoring until the bottom of the ninth inning, when the Giants trailed by three runs. Now the historical tempo dictates a play-by-play account: the Giants score one run on three consecutive hits, and then Bobby Thomson hits a three-run homer to win the game and the pennant.[6] That narrative comprises a full answer to the question; and to repeat, had Hexter described the full season as it really happened, the answer would have been incomprehensible.

6. J. H. Hexter, *The History Primer* (New York, 1971), 149–197.

I cannot hope to improve upon Hexter's analysis, but I can offer a briefer illustration, also from baseball. Leo Durocher, the Giants' manager in 1951, had an uncanny memory: he could, after a game, recapitulate it pitch by pitch. It happens that in the fourth game of the 1929 World Series, the Philadelphia Athletics trailed the Chicago Cubs by eight runs when they came to bat in the seventh inning, whereupon they erupted for ten runs, going on to win ten to eight. Durocher's account of that game—or von Ranke's—would have obscured the excitement and the actual history of that fabulous contest; the whole story is encapsulated in the preceding sentence.

Another example, from another area: in the late 1960s or early 1970s, a time of radical experimentation in the arts, a British producer turned out a movie, *Blowup,* about a London photographer as he goes through his day. He shows up at his studio, takes care of an assortment of things, goes out to a park and takes a number of rapid-fire shots of a fashion model, lunches with somebody, talks business with somebody else, has a dalliance with a pretty girl, and so on. In this perfectly normal day, things happen more at less at random. No meaningful history of this day could be written. But then, in the late afternoon, he goes into his darkroom to develop the shots he had taken that morning. He is curious about a couple of them, and he enlarges one to have a closer look. Something is wrong, and he blows the picture up further. To his amazement, looking in the distance behind the model, he sees that he has photographed a murder taking place. The murder is the story, the possible subject of a history, but it becomes such only when removed from the context of the day's events.

A last example: from 1957 to 1960 Lawrence Durrell published a novel in four volumes, collectively known as *The Alexandria Quartet.* The four are set in Egypt, the first three shortly before the outbreak of World War II, the fourth during the war. The first, *Justine,* recounts a torrid and somewhat twisted affair between a schoolteacher/unsuccessful writer, the narrator, and a beautiful but perverted Jewish woman who is married to a wealthy Coptic banker. A dozen characters populate the story, one of whom, an author named Pursewarden, kills himself. Another, a businessman named Capodistria, is apparently murdered. The Copt has an affair with the narrator's mistress, who has a baby by him, and then he begins to behave quite irrationally. Justine leaves the country to join a kibbutz in Palestine, and on that poignant if mystifying note, the novel ends.

That, as far as the narrator was concerned, is the story as it really happened, but he subsequently learns otherwise. He submits his narrative to a friend, a homosexual physician named Balthazar (for whom the second volume is titled). Balthazar tells him that Justine truly lusted for Pursewarden and that her affair with the narrator was a screen to disguise her real feelings from her husband. This revelation throws the narrator into confusion, causing him to rethink the whole episode and remember matters that he had omitted in his original account. So he tells the tale again—same characters, same place, same time block—but the story is different because it is seen from a different perspective. As Pursewarden wrote in one of his books, "every interpretation of reality is based upon a unique position. Two paces east or west and the whole picture is changed."[7]

Each account is valid from its own perspective, but then we come to the third volume, *Mountolive,* which is told in the third-person, omniscient voice, the voice of the historian, as it were. We learn that neither describes what really happened. Justine, far from being a frivolous and promiscuous woman, is deeply devoted to her husband, with whom she is engaged in a complicated plot to arm the Jews of Palestine, who are to rise in insurrection and force the British and the French to resume an active role in governing the Middle East. That explains the behavior of almost everyone except the original

7. Lawrence Durrell, *The Alexandria Quartet: Justine, Balthazar, Mountolive, Clea* (London, 1969), 210.

narrator, who turns out to have been a pawn in a larger game than he knew existed.

The fourth volume, a sequel, revisits Alexandria a few years later, bringing the characters up-to-date and informing the reader that a number of things in the first three volumes never happened (such as Capodistria's death) and that other things (such as the reason for Pursewarden's suicide) are entirely murky.

These examples necessarily lead us to consider related aspects of what constitutes thinking historically. Historians—whether Everyman, recalling his immediate or distant past, or professionals, attempting to reconstruct the past by studying relics of it—deal in generalizations. To make a generalization is to observe tangible particulars and reduce them to abstractions. Even in considering what is directly and visually observed, that is the process. When we see a tree (and seeing, like remembering, is an acquired ability, not an inherited one), we actually see such of its manifestations as trunk, bark, limbs, and leaves, but we generalize them as "tree"; when we see a number of trees, we generalize them as "woods" or "forest." Similarly, when a historian examines a large number of documents, they are unrelated scraps until the historian, through his own imagination, sees their connections and brings them together. Thus historical thinking not only wrenches the past from context and sequence, it transforms the concrete into the abstract, the discrete into a generalization.

And yet, subjective and artificial as it is, such thinking can communicate an understanding of objective historical reality, much as a map, another contrivance of the imagination, can convey an understanding of objective topographical reality. Whether it does so depends largely upon the level at which the generalization is made. As we live our lives, events unfold simultaneously on a number of levels, from the personal and local to the national and international. The subject matter under investigation dictates both the level of generalization and the questions and data that are relevant to it. Normally these are more obvious to the later investigator than to the participants in the events being investigated, for, though the historian seeks to understand from the participants' points of view, he knows—as they cannot know—how the story comes out. (Remember the cartoon that reads: "Good-bye dear, I'm off to serve in the Hundred Years' War.")

Let us suppose, for example, the subject under study is the history of the United States *as* United States during the early 1770s. The single meaningful question from that perspective was whether, in the imperial crisis, the colonies and the mother country would find a viable way to hold the empire together. And yet, though Americans who followed public affairs knew the empire was troubled, the imperial crisis was not of immediate concern to many until Parliament passed the so-called Intolerable Acts, the Continental Congress convened, and the battles of Lexington and Concord took place. Until then, an ordinary Virginia planter, say, would have been preoccupied with managing his plantation, harvesting and marketing his crops, and similar mundane matters. If the object of the historian's inquiry were tobacco planting and the economics of running a plantation, those would be the stuff of his generalizations. But they would form part of the larger pattern of generalization only if they bore directly on it—as, for example, if planters' concerns about the large sums they owed British merchants impelled them to embrace independence as a way of escaping their debts. (For many, this was what happened.)

Or suppose the historian's subject is religion in eighteenth-century America—specifically, dissenting groups such as the Baptists in Virginia. Baptists were discriminated against not by being forbidden to exercise their religion but by being taxed to support the clergy of the established Church of England. Whether the imperial crisis would form a part of the Baptists' history would, as in the case of the indebted planters, depend upon whether their perceived oppression would induce them to support or oppose the Revolution.

Otherwise, the generalizations germane on a given level have nothing to do with those on a different level.

I shall have a great deal to say about historical thinking during the course of this book, but for now, it seems best to stop and consider the question, of what value is this artificial and abstract way of remembering the past? The answer commonly given is contained in the aphorism, "Those who do not learn from the past are forced to relive it." The remark is more glib than meaningful, for to say that history repeats itself is at best a half truth. Besides, quite apart from the reality that no two situations are ever precisely the same, the wisdom of the observation is mitigated by the record, namely, that the lessons we learn from the past, as individuals and as societies, are as often as not false or harmful lessons. Generals fight the same wars over and over again; ethnic groups are consumed and reconsumed by poisonous hatreds arising from centuries-old grievances.

More positively, thinking historically facilitates our knowing who and where we are. We are the products of our past, and anything that helps us understand what we have been ipso facto helps us understand who we are. Besides, we need orientation, need to know where we are in time as well as in space. On these counts, thinking historically is a preservative of sanity.

But the most valuable characteristic of historical thinking is that, if employed imaginatively, it can enable us to see things around us that would otherwise be invisible—to escape the provincialism of the present. As indicated, when we think historically we try to understand past events and circumstances as the participants did. At first blush that might seem impossible, for it requires seeing through eyes not your own and thinking with a brain other than your own. Careful reflection, however, will indicate that we perform this scientific impossibility as a matter of routine. We know, for instance, what others expect of us, which is not always what we prefer to do, and yet we commonly opt to avoid unpleasantness by doing what is expected. To the extent that we do, we are not only seeing ourselves as others see us—through perceptual apparatuses not our own—but also acting in accordance with the dictates of alien perceptual machinery. To put the matter in a homely fashion, college students encounter professors who teach from points of view (values, assumptions, ideals) that the students do not necessarily share. In such circumstances the intelligent student is able, and usually willing, to write the essays and give the answers the professor wants in order to get a good grade.

The undertaking is of greater difficulty, but the principle is the same in seeking to know how people saw and felt in the past. In this respect, biographies are more instructive for the general reader than is conventional history, for almost every biographer tries to tell the reader what made the subject tick.

Professional historians can fail the laity if they are impelled by contemporary motivations. A large number of them seek to use the past to influence the present. This modus operandi has a history that is the subject of chapter two. For now, suffice it to say that those in search of "a usable past" fall under two broad descriptions. The first are members of groups such as women or ethnic and religious minorities whose history has been neglected and who seek to redress the imbalance. The second are people who wish to further a political or ideological agenda. The one undertaking can be legitimate, the other can never be, but both are plagued by inherent biases, for the historian who scours the record for preconceived answers manages to find them.

The best historians are those who enjoy searching the record of the past for its own sake. I once had a rather dour senior colleague who went into fits of rage when he heard a junior colleague say, as he often did, "I study history because it is fun." But that is precisely the purest motivation possible, and though it does not guarantee accuracy, it is proof against conscious or unconscious warping of the truth.

I can be more specific: the reward of studying the past comes at those moments when, after sifting through piles of documents, one comes to a realization of how the parts fit together into an explanatory generalization. Sometimes the moments come through deliberate and painstaking effort: employing a combination of educated guessing and hit-or-miss analysis, one consciously and logically tries to solve a problem contained in the data, rather in the manner of the detectives in the mystery genre popularized by S. S. Van Dyne, Agatha Christie, Ellery Queen, and Rex Stout. Far more commonly, however, understanding comes spontaneously, out of the blue, for the unconscious mind has been grappling with the problem, and the unconscious can and routinely does make many times more calculations than can be performed on the brain's conscious surface.

I remember vividly the first time I had such an experience on anything resembling a major scale. In January of 1952, I was working at the Microfilm Collection of Early Town Records in the New Hampshire State Library, recording the towns that elected hog reeves, lumber inspectors, and so on, town by town, during the 1780s. I was not looking for anything in particular, but simply following the instructions of my mentor to study everything and take down everything. I had been doing that for the better part of a year, putting in twelve to sixteen hours a day in the historical societies and state archives from Georgia to New Hampshire, living somewhat in a fog. And then, apropos of nothing whatsoever, I had a brilliant insight into a subject entirely unrelated to the documents I was perusing.

In the middle of the 1780s, during a phenomenon historians have described as the paper-money movement, a number of states issued sizable quantities of unsecured paper currency. The conventional accounts of the post-Revolutionary "Critical Period of American History," circa 1781–1789, held that when peace came after Yorktown, American consumers were avid to buy the British goods that had been unavailable since 1775 and bought huge quantities on credit. By the middle of the decade they proved unable to pay for the goods, and a depression set in, whereupon desperate and unprincipled farmer-debtors, led by demagogues, seized control of the state legislatures and issued the paper money for the purpose of paying debts in depreciated currency. The idea that struck me that day in New Hampshire was that the paper money issued in some states, notably Rhode Island, New York, New Jersey, and Pennsylvania, had nothing to do with private indebtedness. Rather, those states were groaning under enormous burdens of *public* debts accumulated to help pay for the war, and their paper money issues represented complicated and sophisticated schemes to service the public debts. I shall not explain here why the realization was important but merely say it warranted alterations in my understanding of the period. The relevant point is that when the insight dawned, it suffused me with indescribable pleasure.

After such moments, one uses one's training to bring to bear the rigorous logical analysis and rechecking of data that should be the standard of professional historians. Sometimes, of course, a brilliant insight turns out to be a half-baked idea. Once while lecturing as a visiting professor at Duke, I had the experience in a wonderful way. I was explaining to the students why Connecticut had serious economic problems during the 1780s. The state's principal export was horses that were sold to sugar plantations in the West Indies. Sailing vessels that carry horses are not, for obvious reasons, suitable for carrying foodstuffs or much of anything else. Connecticut, therefore, imported through its neighboring states, mainly New York and Rhode Island, which taxed them heavily. But in the middle of the lecture I suddenly realized that horse carriers could deal in another cargo—human beings. Connecticuters claimed they had never engaged in the slave trade, but they were not always scrupulously candid. And so, when the lecture ended, my wife and I drove to Columbia, South Carolina, where the state's Department of Archives and History housed the records of every slave imported legally into the United States in the post-Revolutionary period. We made tallies, dutifully noting the points of origin of the slave ships, the owners, and the consignees. As it turned out, not one ship was owned by people in Connecticut. The bright idea had come to naught.

Occasionally, it is impossible to check one's insights, or it seems to be. My most far-fetched moment of understanding in terms of verifiability took place as I was doing research toward a biography of Samuel Insull, the Chicago utilities magnate. I had been studying corporate documents, the records of several government investigations, and similar materials for more than two years. From those sources I had derived a firm understanding of Insull's business career. But my grasp of his personal life left much to be desired. I knew that as a child he had read and been fascinated by the novels of Samuel Smiles, British versions of the rags-to-riches stories written by the American Horatio Alger, and was driven by a determination to be a Success, as Smiles defined the concept. Before his fiftieth birthday Insull had become a Success: he was a millionaire (in pounds sterling, not dollars), he had married a beautiful and talented if somewhat fragile actress, he had sired a healthy and intelligent son, and he was respected in his adopted hometown of Chicago. But I sensed that around his fiftieth year he underwent a fundamental change. Before, he had pursued Success with a single-minded determination and firmly adhered to a maxim he liked to quote, "shoemaker, stick to your last," meaning limit yourself to those activities that you know best. Afterward, he was driven by a craving for power, and he expanded his activities into fields barely related to electric power supply.

At that point I flew from Midway Airport in Chicago to Los Angeles to interview several of Insull's former associates and a man who had been Insull, Jr.'s, closest friend as a child. The only thing I learned that was in any way related to the revelation that was soon to hit me was from the childhood friend, who informed me that during his sixties Insull had kept a mistress. Then I flew back to Chicago on an all-night flight in a noisy propeller-driven DC-7. Unable to sleep, I pondered the interviews I had just had. As we flew over the

Rockies, it suddenly struck me: what had transformed Insull was that his wife had closed the bedroom door, permanently, ending the intimate part of their marriage forever. He had been in his early fifties, an age at which a man's ego wants feeding, an age at which a man's masculinity wants confirmation, an age at which a man can least accommodate rejection. He determined to attain a seat of power so great that he would never be susceptible to rejection again.

Such was the idea, and so overpowered was I by it that after we landed my feet scarcely touched the ground. By the time I had driven home to Madison from Chicago, however, the reality soaked in: the insight lay totally beyond the realm of what could be confirmed. Or that is what I thought.

A week later, I was back in Chicago for further research, and I happened to go to lunch with Insull, Jr. Rather, we went to the Union League Club with the intention of having lunch but stopped off at the bar for a drink, and the lunch never materialized. After several martinis we began talking about my interviews. I mentioned the mistress, whereupon Junior told me an astonishing story. Not long after his father died in 1938, a Chicago newspaper ran a lurid article about Insull and his mistress. After work that day Junior went to see his mother in her North Side apartment, and the two of them consumed a number of martinis. He began to pace the floor, denouncing his father in no uncertain terms, whereupon his mother ordered him to sit down. She said to him, "Junior, I know how you feel. I did not know about it, and believe me it hurts. But you mustn't be too hard on your father. After all, I cut him off in 1912."

Viola! At that moment, I knew that I was a pretty good historian.

Finally, the moments of revelation can come in regard to subjects unrelated to one's current research. I had one about George Washington at a time when my research interests were elsewhere. I had long admired Washington but was uncomfortable with what struck me as melodrama or pretentiousness or something else I could not define. For instance, in his diary during the Constitutional Convention of 1787, he recorded that he was called to the chair but gratuitously added that the vote was unanimous. Diaries are supposed to be for the exclusive use of the diarist, but the entry was made as if Washington were confident that his diaries would become a national treasure, and just in case no one else recorded the fact, he wanted to make sure posterity knew about the unanimity.

The problem was resolved quite by chance. For years, I have read aloud to my wife while she prepares dinner. Our choice of reading matter is eclectic; we simply require the authors to be good prose stylists, and thus we have read all the novels of Charles Dickens and P. G. Wodehouse. Once we were reading Fanny Burney's immensely popular eighteenth-century novel *Cecilia,* the story of a naive country girl who finds herself in London's high society. She is somewhat at a loss until a kindly gentleman at a party points out that everyone present is playing a character—a devil-may-care, a dandy, a wastrel, a wit. When we came to the description my wife and I were immediately smitten with the realization that everybody in public life in the eighteenth century did it. Moreover, it was socially valuable. Given the widespread assumption that man is by nature a rather vile creature, driven by his baser passions, it followed that if one chose a character, like a part in a drama, and played the character long enough and consistently enough, the role became one's "second nature." If the character were noble, one thereby became a better person. We thought of the Americans of the founding generation whom we knew well—from Washington to Jefferson to Franklin to Hamilton to Adams—and we realized every one of them played characters, sometimes a variety of roles. The feeling that Washington was acting a role or playing on the stage of history was sound. He was. And the contrivance benefited mankind.[8]

8. Fanny Burney, *Cecilia; or Memoirs of an Heiress* (London, 1782). The role of character has increasingly informed studies of historical figures. See, for example, Kenneth A. Lockridge, *The Diary, and Life, of William Byrd II of Virginia, 1674–1744* (Chapel Hill, N.C., 1987), 21–24 and passim; Richard Brookhiser,

Having such experiences is what justifies my junior colleague's declaration that history is fun. But another side of the game is not fun, at least for me, and that is writing it up—a task of increased difficulty because in history, as opposed to other disciplines, the common outlet for writing is books, not articles. Just how much fun writing history books is *not* is demonstrated by the fact that few historians actually do it. To be sure, because historians in America normally earn their livings as college professors and because a Ph.D. is normally required for entry into the profession, practitioners must have written at least a book-length work as their doctoral dissertation. But barely one in five dissertations is subsequently revised and published, and even if the dissertation is published, the vast majority of professional historians stop there.

I could offer any number of case studies. When I was a newcomer in the game, I met a historian who was fairly well known as the man who was going to write the definitive history of the First Bank of the United States. He studied the subject for years, became a mine of information, and took his knowledge to the grave, for he never wrote the book. My own mentor, Fulmer Mood, was anointed as the biographer of Frederick Jackson Turner; after twenty years of waiting, the frontier historian Ray Allen Billington concluded that Mood would never produce the biography and wrote one himself. My friend Thomas P. Govan was a walking encyclopedia of understanding of the American past, and he published a number of articles that were pure gems, but he wrote only one post-dissertation book during a long career, a masterful biography of Nicholas Biddle.

Alexander Hamilton: American (New York, 1999); Paul K. Longmore, *The Invention of George Washington* (Berkeley, Calif., 1988); Barry Schwartz, *George Washington: The Making of an American Symbol* (New York, 1987); Forrest McDonald, "Washington, Cato, and Honor: A Model for Revolutionary Leadership," in *American Models of Revolutionary Leadership: George Washington and Other Founders,* ed. Daniel J. Elazar and Ellis Katz (Lanham, Md., 1992), 43–58; Esmond Wright, *Franklin of Philadelphia* (Cambridge, Mass., 1987). See also the appendix.

Among those who do write throughout their lives, two sets of motivations are at work. The first set is practical and is encapsulated in the aphorism "publish or perish." History professors are supposed both to perform in the classroom and to write books. What it takes to do these discrete operations is a split personality, for the one requires an extrovert who expects and receives instant gratification for his efforts, whereas the other is a lonely, introverted activity in which the rewards are deferred for years. Whether the system is fair is beside the point, though I personally believe the truly productive writers are the best teachers. Be that as it may, rewards in the profession are usually based on the quality and quantity of one's publications. A young Ph.D. takes his first teaching job at a small college; if he hopes to find employment elsewhere, he must publish his way there. And at any institution, raises and promotions depend upon published writings, not what one does before live students.[9]

The other motivations are moral and are wrapped in the concept of the scholarly ideal. In the abstract, scholars in any discipline seek to know for the sake of knowing, and they form a community whose membership extends over the ages, each making a contribution toward the expansion of human knowledge and understanding. More tangibly, the scholar seeks knowledge because it provides pleasure, but that selfish pleasure entails obligations. I can do what I do because Jared Sparks gathered documents about the Revolution and Founding, and because Lyman C. Draper rode horseback though the backcountry to gather documents for the State Historical Society of Wisconsin even before Wisconsin became a state, and because J. Franklin Jameson collected manuscripts for deposit and classification in the Library of Congress. I can do what I do because thousands of curators and librarians have gathered and sorted buildingsful of treasures, and because editors have collected and pub-

9. For a sometimes supporting and sometimes contrary appraisal, see Theodore Hamerow, *Reflections on History and Historians* (Madison, Wis., 1987), 95, 108–111, 136–139, 141–143.

lished volumes of original sources, and because historians during the course of more than two centuries have studied and written about what they have learned.

I owe these people, as well as my teachers, an enormous debt of gratitude for what they have done for me, but they are dead and gone. The only way I can pay my debt to them is to pass along the understanding I have obtained, so future scholars can learn from my efforts. They, in turn, are obliged to repay me by passing along that understanding, enriched by their own studies and thought, to generations yet to come.

TWO

∎

The World as I Entered It

When I entered graduate school at the University of Texas, the history department was scarcely cosmopolitan. Only one of its members attended the meetings of the major historical associations, and none talked about the philosophy of history, at least not to students. Such influential American historians as Frederick Jackson Turner, Carl Becker, and Charles A. Beard were given cursory treatment. We all learned something about Turner and his frontier thesis, to be sure, for on the faculty was an eminent frontier historian, Walter Prescott Webb; but Webb was by no means a disciple of Turner, and indeed, he insisted that he had never even heard of Turner's celebrated frontier essay until long after he had been publishing works on the West. As for Beard, Eugene Campbell Barker, the Grand Old Man of Texas history, launched into anti-Beardian diatribes at the very mention of his name. And as for Becker, I do not believe I ever heard anyone mention him.

As a consequence, I emerged from graduate school entirely ignorant of what had been happening in the profession over the course of the preceding three or four decades. Two developments in particular would form the milieu in which, as a historian, I would work. The first concerned the philosophy of history, the profession's understanding of what it was about: the subjective-relativist-presentist point of view. In a nutshell, this was the notion that all judgments are subjective, all observations are relative to the point of view of the observer, and all historians study and write, consciously or unconsciously, with an eye toward influencing the present and the future.

The other was the so-called New History, study of the past on the assumption that economic forces underlie and condition political and social events. And, whereas I could be blissfully ignorant of the subjective-relativist-presentist philosophy until after I had finished my graduate work, I was infused, willy-nilly, with the interpretive work of the New History—save for Barker's anti-Beardian screeds—for that work permeated every textbook and each lecture.

Against this backdrop, my career began.

In an 1891 essay Frederick Jackson Turner offered the heretical suggestion that *"each age writes the history of the past anew with reference to the conditions uppermost in its own time"* [italics in the original]. Few of his contemporaries in academe would have agreed, clinging instead to a Germanic belief in scientific objectivity and a faith in progress. To them, if past and present were related, the connection was quite the reverse: the past shed light on the present in the sense that "what is past is prologue."[1]

Before Turner died four decades later, American historians had come to accept his dictum as a commonplace. The path toward acceptance was erratic, and resistance was often stubborn, but by the time Carl Becker delivered his 1931 presidential address before the American Historical Association, "Everyman His Own Historian," and Charles A. Beard followed two years later with his "Written

1. Patricia Nelson Limerick, "Turnerians All: The Dream of a Helpful History in an Intelligible World," *American Historical Review* 100 (1995): 697–716, quote at 704. See also Wilbur R. Jacobs, ed., *Frederick Jackson Turner's Legacy* (San Marino, Calif., 1965).

History as an Act of Faith," the subjective-relativist-presentist position was regarded as received wisdom.

Various factors contributed to the change of outlook. Not least was Turner's influence as an educator, for his teachings cast a spell over his students. The truly potent instrument for change, however, was experience: the rapid transformation of American social and political concerns and institutions and—most traumatically—the activity of leading historians during World War I. On that occasion the profession put its patriotism before its pursuit of truth. For what they considered a higher cause, American historians sold out. Afterward, it was but a short step to rationalize what had been done and to profess that, as mortals, historians could do no other.

Before the war, if one may judge by the annual addresses of the presidents of the American Historical Association, American historians believed themselves to be objective scientists whose work was of value mainly in shaping good, patriotic citizens. But these addresses, simultaneously naive and smug, were reflective of the attitudes of upper-class America, and they were already coming under siege. Beard, as a young associate professor of politics and history at Columbia, had recently spent time in Manchester, England, observing the travails of the working class, and he returned to America convinced that struggles between economic groups underlay the political developments of the preceding centuries. In 1907–1908 he joined forces with James Harvey Robinson to publish a two-volume work, *The Development of Modern Europe,* in which they spurned the traditional emphasis on wars and politics and stressed economic and social developments as the "real" driving forces in history. "It has been their ever-conscious aim," the writers declared, "to enable the reader to catch up with his own times; to read intelligently the foreign news in the morning papers." In 1912 Robinson went a step further, arguing in *The New History* that Rankean "objective" history was both impossible and undesirable.[2]

2. Harvey Wish, *The American Historian: A Social-Intellectual History of the Writing of the American Past* (New York, 1960), 268–269.

Almost immediately, presidents of the American Historical Association joined the chorus. In 1914 Andrew C. McLaughlin, a distinguished constitutional historian, professed his faith in objectivity but added that history was ever-changing because present preoccupations were always in flux. Consequently, history was necessarily written to serve the current interests of the historian. A year later, H. Morse Stephens advanced similar arguments, though he urged honest historians to attempt to overcome their presentist biases while recognizing the impossibility of doing so.[3]

Subjectivism-relativism-presentism was catching on, and the experience of World War I accelerated the process. Historians took part in the war effort at the behest of one of their own number, President Woodrow Wilson. As a professional historian, Wilson was aware that Americans had been bitterly divided during previous wars, and when the United States entered the Great War in 1917 he was determined that for once the people must stand together. Moreover, Wilson was a man with a rigidly uncompromising psyche, and he could imagine no war but an all-out war.

"It is a fearful thing to lead this great peaceful people into war, into the most terrible and disastrous of all wars," he declared in his message to Congress, "civilization itself seeming to be in the balance." Prosecuting it successfully, he believed, would hinge upon the creation of a "proper war spirit," by which he meant dedication bordering on the hysterical.[4] To an extent such a spirit arose more or less spontaneously, though at every step along the way the hysteria was fanned by State Councils of Defense that policed and prodded it, down to the establishment of neighborhood watchdog groups.

3. Andrew C. McLaughlin, "American History and American Democracy," *American Historical Review* 20 (1915): 255–276, quote at 258; H. Morse Stephens, "Nationality and History," *American Historical Review* 21 (1916): 225–236.

4. Woodrow Wilson, "Speech for Declaration of War against Germany," April 2, 1917, in *Documents of American History*, 7th ed., ed. Henry Steele Commager (New York, 1963), 2: 132.

Much of what was done was petty, albeit vicious: some German Americans were stoned or tarred and feathered; schools stopped teaching German; the name of sauerkraut was changed to liberty cabbage; frankfurters became liberty sausages; the playing of Beethoven and Wagner was prohibited. Some actions, however, were not petty. In July of 1918, for instance, vigilance committees in Chicago seized and searched 150,000 men, held 20,000 of them in jails and warehouses, and triumphantly announced that 14 of these men were draft dodgers.[5]

The principal agency charged with "holding fast the inner lines" was the Committee on Public Information, headed by former newspaperman George Creel. The Creel committee saw to it that every American who read anything about the war, whether in a big-city daily newspaper or in a country weekly, read exactly the same thing from exactly the same angle. It was "voluntary," for the committee merely supplied the materials and exercised no direct censorship, though anyone who dared to print a different version risked running afoul of draconian penalties prescribed by law.[6]

In addition to propagandizing through print, the committee reached people directly through the spoken word—an impressive feat, inasmuch as the first radio broadcast did not take place until nearly two years after the war. The instrumentality was the Four-Minute Men, speakers who were recruited across the nation to deliver simultaneously identical four-minute speeches in theaters, schools, and churches. At the peak, 75,000 speakers were thus engaged in "broadcasting without a radio," delivering speeches to what Creel estimated to be a total audience of 400 million.[7]

5. Marguerite E. Jenison, ed., *The War Time Organization of Illinois* (Springfield, Ill., 1923), 29–66; Forrest McDonald, Leslie E. Decker, and Thomas P. Govan, *The Last Best Hope: A History of the United States* (Reading, Mass., 1973), 750–751.

6. James R. Mock and Cedric Larson, *Words That Won the War: The Story of the Committee on Public Information, 1917–1919* (Princeton, N.J., 1939), 4.

7. Ibid., 125, 113–130, passim; Forrest McDonald, *Insull* (Chicago, 1962), 170–172.

But for President Wilson that was not enough: as a historian, he regarded it as essential to control what Americans thought about the past. Accordingly, a Division of Civic and Educational Cooperation, better known as the history subcommittee, was established. The director was Guy Stanton Ford of the University of Minnesota, a scholar of German history who would become president of both his institution and the American Historical Association. The list of historians who wrote propagandistic history for the division reads like a scholars' all-star team: Andrew C. McLaughlin, Evarts B. Greene, J. Franklin Jameson, Frederick L. Paxson, Dana C. Munro, Frederick Jackson Turner, William E. Dodd, Carl Becker, and Charles A. Beard.[8]

The output of this group was staggering. The authors ground out a hundred books and pamphlets, each of them attaining a circulation that few historians could ever achieve in their scholarly work. A pamphlet on Germany's supposed war aims, coauthored by five historians, had a circulation of 6,813,340 copies. A series of "Loyalty Leaflets" had an average distribution of half a million copies. All told, the division put out 75 million pieces of propaganda. And as if that were not enough, it published a periodical, *National School Service,* which reached 20 million homes. A monthly *History Teacher's Magazine,* sent to history teachers, included as a regular feature "Timely Suggestions for Secondary School History" to make sure the nation's children were being instilled with a proper war spirit.[9]

The content of these publications ranged from almost truthful to wildly distorted. The general message was that Britain and France had always been friendly toward each other and toward America, being devoted champions of freedom and democracy, and that Germany had always been their brutally tyrannical enemy who aspired to rule the world and stamp out freedom. A number of discrepancies in that version of the past were difficult to get around: England

8. Mock and Larson, *Words That Won the War,* 158–186; Forrest McDonald, "Charles A. Beard," in *Pastmasters: Some Essays on American Historians,* ed. Marcus Cunliffe and Robin W. Winks (New York, 1969), 433 nn. 44, 45.

9. Mock and Larson, *Words That Won the War,* chap. 7.

and France had been blood enemies for centuries; Britain did rule a large portion of the world with an iron hand; England and Prussia had been traditionally allied against France. Most embarrassing for the committee was the American Revolution, in which France had joined the United States in a war to remove the British yoke. The historians solved that problem ingeniously. Americans and the British had devoutly loved one another, the new account went, but Britain unfortunately came under the control of a mad German king who aspired to destroy liberty in both places and attempted to suppress the Americans by hiring German mercenaries.

The revised version ran up against the stubborn physical fact that hundreds of thousands of existing textbooks told a different story. Professors and high school teachers overcame this little snag by systematically combing the textbooks and physically removing, with scissors, each favorable reference to Germany or Germans and any statement running counter to the patriotic party line.

What the profession had done clearly called for justification. This Lost Generation of historians needed an authoritative voice or voices to say to them, "There, there. It's nobody's fault. You're human, and therefore you can't help yourselves." It found those voices in Carl Becker and Charles A. Beard.

When Becker delivered his Everyman address, he had in press *The Heavenly City of the Eighteenth-Century Philosophers,* in which he developed his subjectivist-relativist ideas at considerable length. In the book he pointed out that the New History was an ancient and recurring phenomenon. Saint Augustine had devised a New History in the fifth century, Becker declared, as had the humanists a millennium later and the philosophes in the eighteenth century. He insisted that history had always been propaganda in service of ideology, consciously or unconsciously.[10]

10. Carl Becker, *The Heavenly City of the Eighteenth-Century Philosophers* (New Haven, Conn., 1932).

In the Everyman address Becker explained, in a roundabout way, why each generation perceives the past in accordance with the changing preoccupations of changing times—what he called the "climate of opinion." He began by defining history as "the memory of things said and done," as opposed to things actually said and done. Everyman has memories of things said and done, needs them to preserve his sanity, and regularly does research of a sort to verify or correct his memory. For the professional historian as well as Everyman, this memory of things said and done is an imaginative recreation, woven "at the behest of circumstance and purpose."[11]

The scientific historians had thought otherwise, believing that they could do pure research, digging up fact after fact until the sources were exhausted and the facts would "speak for themselves." This was "an illusion," Becker told his audience, itself the product of the nineteenth-century zeitgeist. "Hoping to find something without looking for it . . . was surely the most romantic species of realism yet invented, the oddest attempt ever made to get something for nothing!"[12] But according to Becker, the current generation was outgrowing that silly conceit.

Becker might, however, be accused here of the logical fallacy of assuming what he intended to prove. By postulating that the student of the past begins with a question and a reason for wanting to know the answer, he has predetermined the outcome of the investigation. As various historians have commented, if one looks for something specific in the record, that is what one will find. Becker did not allow for investigators who looked at the record for its own sake, out of sheer curiosity, not caring what they found.

But Becker had an answer to such objections. The proper function of historians was ages-old, preserving the myths for the benefit of Mr. Everyman, albeit with higher critical standards than the ancient

11. Carl Becker, "Everyman His Own Historian," *American Historical Review* 37 (1932): 221–236, quotes at 223, 230.

12. Ibid., 232, 233.

bards. "Otherwise," Mr. Everyman "will leave us to our own devices, leave us it may be to cultivate a species of dry professional arrogance growing out of the thin soil of antiquarian research." Research of that sort "will be of little import except in so far as it is transmuted into common knowledge. The history that lies inert in unread books does no work in the world." And when we write for Mr. Everyman, we cannot "impose our version of the human story" on him; rather, he "imposes his version on us—compelling us, in an age of political revolution, to see that history is past politics, in an age of social stress and conflict to search for the economic interpretation."[13]

Near the end of the address, Becker added with characteristic irony, "I do not present this view of history as one that is stable and must prevail. Whatever validity it may claim, it is certain, on its own premises, to be supplanted."[14]

Up to a point, Charles A. Beard in his "Written History as an Act of Faith" said pretty much what Becker had said, though he was more forceful and direct. Like Becker, Beard began with a definition of history. History is "contemporary thought about . . . past actuality, instructed and delimited by history as record and knowledge . . . authenticated by criticism and ordered with the help of the scientific method."[15]

Everybody knows, Beard continued, that the historian "is a product of his age, and that his work reflects the spirit of the times, of a nation, race, group, class, or section," and that historians are "influenced in their selection and ordering of materials by their biases, prejudices, beliefs, affections, general upbringing, and experience." We know this to be "true," Beard said, because "every written history . . . is a selection and arrangement of facts" by "an act of choice,

13. Ibid., 234, 235.
14. Ibid., 235, 236.
15. Charles A. Beard, "Written History as an Act of Faith," *American Historical Review* 39 (1934): 219–229, quotes at 219, 220. Lee Benson, *Turner and Beard, American Historical Writing Reconsidered* (Glencoe, Ill., 1960).

conviction, and interpretation respecting values."[16] (The last words are the chiller.)

Contemporary thought therefore rejected the scientific school's premise that the past could be described as it actually was. Rejection of the Rankean formula arose from challenges by professional historians and from the ongoing movement of history itself. Historians tried to proceed as if they were physical scientists, but their subject matter did not permit it. Beard offered as an aside that if history were reduced to formulas we would have a godlike knowledge of the future, and "humanity would have nothing to do except to await its doom." He next suggested relativity but, as Becker had done, dismissed that as self-annihilating.[17]

Now Beard went beyond Becker. He declared that historians must consider the totality of historical occurrences in one of three ways. History is chaos, history moves in cycles, or history "is moving in some direction away from the low level of primitive beginnings, on an upward gradient toward a more ideal order." None of these is entirely satisfactory, but the historian must choose one as "an act of faith." "And the degree of his influence and immortality will depend upon the length and correctness of his forecast—upon the verdict of history yet to come."[18]

The historian must recognize "that any selection and arrangement of facts . . . is controlled inexorably by the frame of reference in the mind of the selector and arranger," including "things deemed necessary, things deemed possible, and things deemed desirable." Faced by these facts, the historian can attempt to "evade them," or he can "examine his own frame of reference," seek to clarify and expand it, "and give it consistency." Beard's guess as to the desirable and probable movement of history was that it was toward "a collectivist democracy."[19]

16. Beard, "Written History as an Act of Faith," 220.
17. Ibid., 224.
18. Ibid., 226.
19. Ibid., 227–228.

* * *

The historical fraternity had found absolution for its sins, and for sins to come.[20] But some dissenting voices were heard. In 1935 T. C. Smith published an article in the *American Historical Review* in which he took Beard to task, not for holding that objectivity was unattainable but for suggesting that it was undesirable. A Beardian misuse of history for propaganda purposes, Smith noted, was precisely what was then taking place in fascist Italy, Nazi Germany, and communist Russia, and Beard's doctrine invited such abuse in America.[21]

A scholar of the constitutional history of England, C. H. McIlwain, made a related point in his presidential address before the American Historical Association in 1936. McIlwain noted the logical flaw in arguing that because we cannot know the whole story of the past with certainty, we can know none of it, and therefore we should not bother to try. As for enriching history by bringing present conceptions to bear upon it, McIlwain remarked that valuable recent reinterpretations in his field came not from modern viewpoints but from shedding such viewpoints and rediscovering "frames of reference" that had prevailed in the past and were thus relevant to the subjects at hand.[22]

In 1946 the brilliant if eccentric historian of Kansas James C. Malin—who had taken Becker's course on the French Revolution during Becker's last semester of teaching at the University of Kansas—levied a formidable volley of blasts at the Beard-Becker dicta. Malin repeated and embellished the criticisms made by Smith and McIlwain; assailed Beard's three-ways-of-seeing-history model as a closed system, whereas history is open; and attacked the notion that one begins with an inquiry or a hypothesis, which underlay the

20. James C. Malin, *Essays on Historiography* (Ann Arbor, Mich., 1948), 116–117.

21. Theodore Clarke Smith, "The Writing of American History in America, from 1884 to 1934," *American Historical Review* 40 (1935): 439–449.

22. C. H. McIlwain, "The Historian's Part in a Changing World," *American Historical Review* 42 (1937): 207–224.

thinking of Becker and Beard. Malin's teacher F. W. Hodder (who ironically had been a student and admirer of Becker) taught that "history should be studied as it is lived, as a whole, and that the most realistic approach was to select a period and then work it intensively." According to this approach, the historian would "place himself in the age chosen for study, and . . . endeavor to develop the story, to recreate its unfolding as it appeared to the actors of that era." Malin described at length how he had followed that method in doing the research for his work *John Brown and the Legend of Fifty-six*, in which it was impossible for present preoccupations to enter the study.[23]

And Samuel Eliot Morison, in his 1950 presidential address, lambasted Beard while describing his own faith as a historian. Beard, he said, "sets up a straw Ranke who pretended to reproduce past 'actuality' in toto, and in a syllogism that makes one gasp for breath, goes on to assert that, since no historian can escape his personal limitations or transcend those of space and time, he must so select and arrange the facts of history as to influence the present or future in the direction that *he* considers socially desirable."[24]

These were powerful criticisms and potent critics, but they were minority voices. When I entered the game in 1949, Beard and Becker were in the ascendancy, and the New History reigned supreme. The subjective-relativists rewrote American history from end to end, but despite their contempt for what Beard called "barren political history," they still organized the subject around political developments, thus keeping the Federalist Era, the Age of Jackson, the Civil War and Reconstruction, the Progressive Era, and so on.

On that traditional frame, however, they wove a different tapestry. For them the driving force was economic rivalry between

23. Malin, *Essays,* 141–168, quotes at 149, 143.
24. Samuel Eliot Morison, "Faith of a Historian," *American Historical Review* 56 (1951): 261–275, quote at 266.

contending groups of good guys and bad guys. Arrayed in the good-guys camp were farmers, debtors, frontiersmen, laborers, the poor, and their reform-minded leaders. Among the bad guys were merchants, manufacturers, owners of transportation facilities and utilities, speculators, and the well-off in general, together with the reactionary political hacks who toadied to them. The struggle was endless; sometimes one group won, sometimes the other, but ultimately the good guys were destined to triumph.

The prevailing interpretation of seventeenth-century America was largely the work of an erstwhile Kansas populist turned literature professor at the University of Washington, Vernon L. Parrington. His first book, *Main Currents of American Thought,* was published in two volumes in 1927. It was bold, sweeping, opinionated, and wildly inaccurate. Accordingly, it won the Pulitzer Prize for history and was immensely popular. Selecting his literary figures carefully and culling their works for quotations that buttressed his points, Parrington depicted the Puritans as rigid, stern proto-capitalists whose pretended piety was a ploy to oppress their inferiors under a Calvinist yoke. He pulled no punches in his descriptions. Of Cotton Mather, for example, Parrington wrote, "What a crooked and diseased mind lay back of those eyes that were forever spying out occasions to magnify self. . . . His egoism blots out charity and even the divine mercy."[25]

The few good guys among the Yankees were the likes of Roger Williams and Anne Hutchinson, who rebelled against the Puritan oligarchs and established a forerunner of Jeffersonian democracy. To Parrington that was truly good, for he idolized Jefferson as "a perennial inspiration. A free soul, he loved freedom enough to deny it to none." Overlooking Jefferson's ownership of human beings, Parrington honest-to-God said that. Despite that appraisal, little of

25. Ralph H. Gabriel, "Vernon Louis Parrington," in *Pastmasters,* 143.

Virginia appeared in the colonial volume of *Main Currents,* for Virginia had not yet evolved into a Jeffersonian paradise.[26]

The New History's account of the coming of the Revolution was based largely upon Carl Becker's doctoral dissertation, written under Turner and published in 1909 as *The History of Political Parties in the Province of New York, 1760–1776.* When embellished by others it served as the Revised Standard Version of the advent of the Revolution. New York politics was dominated by great aristocratic families, the Hudson River patroons, and by their counterparts in the city, international importing merchants. When troubles with England began, New York was particularly hard hit, and the patroons and the merchants led the resistance. As time passed, however, leaders of the lower orders began to emerge, violence erupted, and radical reforms loomed. On the eve of independence, the radicals took over; the aristocrats became Loyalists. The Revolution in New York was thus a dual struggle, one for "home rule" and the other to determine who should rule at home.

The New History assumed that after 1776 New York continued to be democratized as the landed estates of the Tory aristocrats were confiscated and presumably sold in small parcels to former tenants. Arthur Schlesinger extended Becker's thesis to apply elsewhere in *The Colonial Merchants and the American Revolution* (1918), and J. Franklin Jameson rounded out the interpretation in *The American Revolution Considered as a Social Movement* (1926), postulating that a nationwide process of democratization took place.

Following logically from this reading, the creation of the Constitution was not the fulfillment of the Revolution but something in the nature of a counterrevolution. A Turner student, Orin G. Libby, showed that the contest over ratification had pitted coastal Federalist regions against rural anti-Federalist regions and concluded that,

26. Ibid., 144.

inasmuch as the coastal areas were commercial and the backcountry was populated by small farmers, the struggle was primarily economic. Another Turner student, the avowed Marxist Algie Simons, went further, declaring that "the organic law of this nation was formulated in secret session by a body called into existence through a conspiratory trick and was forced upon a disfranchised people by means of a dishonest apportionment in order that the interests of a small body of wealthy rulers might be served."[27]

When Beard built upon these obscure works to write his blockbuster *An Economic Interpretation of the Constitution of the United States* (1913), a whole nation was stunned.

Beard's interpretation was based upon the assumption that the decade of the 1780s had been a period of widespread depression and commercial stagnation. Financial chaos set in, certificates of the massive public debt issued to pay for the war became virtually worthless, and state legislatures, under the sway of demagogues and dishonest debtors, inundated the country with worthless paper money. During the winter of 1786–1787 debtor hordes assembled in western Massachusetts under the leadership of Captain Daniel Shays and threatened a general redistribution of property.

In these circumstances, according to Beard, "Large and important groups of economic interests were adversely affected by the system of government under the Articles of Confederation, namely, those of public securities, shipping and manufacturing, money at interest; in short, capital as opposed to land." Being unable to protect their property, these "personalty" groups called a convention in the hope of obtaining "the adoption of a revolutionary programme." Small farmers and debtors, though the mass of the population, were

27. Wish, *American Historian,* 267. The historians E. R. A. Seligman and J. Allen Smith had written pretty much the same thing as Simons. Libby's 1894 dissertation was titled "Geographical Distribution of the Vote of the Thirteen States on the Ratification of the Federal Constitution, 1787–1788."

excluded from participation. The Constitution was the work of men who were, "with a few exceptions, immediately, directly, and personally interested in, and derived economic advantage from, the establishment of the new system." The Constitution was "an economic document drawn with superb skill" and was based "upon the concept that the fundamental private rights of property are anterior in government and morally beyond the reach of popular majorities."[28]

During the contest for ratification, personalty interests gained the upper hand by disfranchising opponents, and the basis of division was economic. Supporters of ratification were centered (as Libby had pointed out) "particularly in the regions in which mercantile, manufacturing, security, and personalty interests generally had their greatest strength." Those who held public securities "formed a very considerable dynamic element, if not the preponderating element, in bringing about" ratification. Opposition arose in agricultural regions and in areas where debtors had agitated for paper money and related debt-avoidance schemes. In sum, "the line of cleavage for and against the Constitution was between substantial personalty interests on the one hand and the small farming and debtor interests on the other."[29]

Reaction to the book was widespread and vociferous. Traditionalists were outraged: future president Warren G. Harding, editorializing in his *Marion* (Ohio) *Star,* grew almost apoplectic in his denunciation, and former president William Howard Taft, in public speeches, was nearly as vehement, though reputedly Taft privately remarked, "Of course it is true, but the damned fool shouldn't have been allowed to publish it." Progressives were equally unreserved in their praise. Angered by recent Supreme Court decisions that had struck down treasured reforms, they applauded Beard because they

28. Forrest McDonald, *We the People: The Economic Origins of the Constitution* (Chicago, 1958), 4–5; Charles A. Beard, *An Economic Interpretation of the Constitution of the United States* (New York, 1913), 63, 188, 324.

29. McDonald, *We the People,* 6; Beard, *Economic Interpretation,* 290, 291, 325.

believed his work would help undermine what they regarded as excessive veneration of the Constitution. The leading academic journals lauded Beard warmly.

Within five years, Beard's interpretation was making its way into the textbooks—a process that normally took longer—and for four decades thereafter it was generally accepted. By the end of World War II the book had been reprinted fifteen times.

Beard published a follow-up volume that became the conventional account of the origins of the American party system. The long-held understanding as described in John S. Bassett's *The Federalist System* (1906) maintained that after ratification, domestic harmony prevailed; permanent divisions arose in response to Hamilton's fiscal program. Orin Libby put forth a more formidable argument employing methods similar to those he had used in regard to ratification and adding a careful analysis of voting in Congress during the 1790s. He concluded that no regular party system had materialized before 1798; parties crystallized at that time in response to the Alien and Sedition Acts and the Quasi-War with France.

Not so, Beard argued in *Economic Origins of Jeffersonian Democracy* (1915). He disposed of Bassett and Libby contemptuously and staked out his position that the alignments during ratification remained essentially intact after 1788, the sole significant shift being that southern plantation owners recognized that their interests were closer to the agrarian anti-Federalists than to the capitalistic Federalists who had been their allies. The agrarian coalition fought the capitalists for more than a decade before triumphing in the election of 1800.

Beard's rendition of the origins of Jeffersonian democracy came to be as accepted as his interpretation of the Constitution; Libby and his work were eclipsed. Libby spent his entire career teaching at the University of North Dakota. Given his early and well-received publications, he should have received a call from a prestigious university, but no call was forthcoming. If one can credit hearsay evidence, Libby's obscurity was due to sinister forces. Late in his life, he told my mentor, Fulmer Mood, that Beard had systematically thwarted every opportunity Libby had to better his position.

Beard indicated in a footnote to *Economic Origins* that he intended to write "a fuller review of the political economy of the Republicans after the inaugural of Jefferson," but he never did so, nor did any other New Historian. Partly, no doubt, they were daunted by the towering work of Henry Adams. A more potent deterrent was that they could not reconcile Jefferson's presidency with their image of Jefferson. Accordingly, they ignored the subject.[30]

They did not, however, overlook the ensuing Era of Good Feelings. The period won its name by virtue of the collapse of the Federalists as a party, but in practice, feelings were rancorous, and a wave of nationalistic legislation topped anything the Federalists had enacted. Corruption grew apace. Congress recreated the Bank of the United States and passed a protective tariff at the expense of honest farmers. Furthermore, Congress was profligate in appropriating money for internal improvements and spent lavishly on a permanent army and navy, in violation of cherished Jeffersonian principles.

The Second Bank of the United States was the true heavy in the New Historians' story. Its first president, William Jones of Philadelphia, had been chosen for purely political reasons, and under his incompetent management the Bank grossly overextended itself. A general economic collapse came with the Panic of 1819. Prices plummeted, unemployment infested the nation's cities, and tens of thousands of farmers had their land sold for debts as the Bank ruthlessly foreclosed their mortgages. As the panic subsided, the Bank was taken over by the diabolically competent Nicholas Biddle. Biddle's

---

30. Charles A. Beard, *Economic Origins of Jeffersonian Democracy* (New York, 1915), 440. For the non-Jeffersonian aspects of Jefferson's presidency, see Forrest McDonald, *The Presidency of Thomas Jefferson* (Lawrence, Kans., 1976), 139–169. For an informed appraisal of Jeffersonians in economic terms, see Drew R. McCoy, *The Elusive Republic: Political Economy in Jeffersonian America* (Chapel Hill, N.C., 1980).

very competence, in the eyes of the good guys, made the Bank more monstrous. Steadily and progressively, Biddle brought the entire banking system under his personal control and kept powerful politicians—Daniel Webster, for instance—on his payroll.

Compounding the nation's woes, the political order broke down. Since the triumph of Jefferson in 1800, the franchise had been broadened enormously, and the barriers the capitalists-Federalists had erected against the demos were no longer efficacious. Accordingly, in 1824 the presidential election was truly democratic. Andrew Jackson received a plurality of the popular votes, but no candidate had a majority of the electoral votes. As a result, the election went to the House of Representatives, whereupon Speaker of the House Henry Clay made "the Corrupt Bargain" with Adams and delivered the presidency to him in exchange for the secretaryship of state.

Though Adams had long before switched from his father's party and become a Jeffersonian Republican, when he assumed the presidency he proved to be a greater nationalist than even Hamilton had been. His term in office was a calamity, reaching its nadir in the passage of the Tariff of Abominations in 1828. Fortunately, the Jacksonians used the four years to organize, thus ensuring that the man of the people would sweep to victory in 1828.

The New History's account of Jacksonian democracy was largely the coinage of Frederick Jackson Turner and his disciples, but it was strikingly Beardian in its lineup of heroes and villains. The good guys were those who had lost out in 1787–1788, the frontier farmers, joined by small agriculturalists elsewhere—the individualistic, self-reliant, egalitarian majority, as depicted in Turner's *The Rise of the New West, 1819–1829*. The bad guys were those who had pulled off the coup of 1787, moneyed men, merchants, manufacturers, speculators, holders of the public debt, and denizens of the seaport cities. The Jacksonians' task was to break their hold and return control of the common man's life to the common man.

Jackson's greatest triumph over the vested interests was his destruction of the Second Bank. He declared in his inaugural address that the Bank was unconstitutional, despite a Supreme Court ruling to the contrary; he took the Jeffersonian position that each branch of the federal government had equal authority to judge the constitutionality of acts of Congress. When the Bank was prematurely rechartered in 1832, Jackson delivered a powerful veto message. He denounced Congress for passing legislation designed to make "the rich richer and the potent more powerful." Such legislation, he said, was a "prostitution of our government to the advancement of the few at the expense of the many." He accused the Bank of arraying "section against section, interest against interest, and man against man, in a fearful commotion"—which was in truth what Jackson himself had been doing.[31]

Less dramatic but quite as effective was Jackson's shutting off the internal improvements boondoggle. In May 1830, Congress authorized a federal subscription for building a sixty-mile stretch of road in Kentucky. Jackson vetoed the Maysville Road bill, because the road was inside the limits of a single state (coincidentally, the home state of one of his dearest enemies).

Jackson's stand in regard to the tariff involved him in a larger controversy. Though he agreed that the 1828 Tariff of Abominations should be repealed, he was concerned lest a drastic tariff cut interfere with his hope of paying off the public debt. (This was a cherished goal that he succeeded in accomplishing.) A complication arose when, after Congress lowered the tariffs somewhat in 1832, South Carolina followed a doctrine coined by Vice President John C. Calhoun and called a convention to declare the tariffs of 1828 and 1832 null and void. People simply did not defy Andrew Jackson. He ordered preparations for invading the state and proclaimed that refusing to obey federal law was treason. The showdown did

31. Forrest McDonald, *States' Rights and the Union: Imperium in Imperio, 1776–1876* (Lawrence, Kans., 2000), 112.

not occur, however, for Henry Clay formulated a compromise bill to reduce the tariff in phases, and the crisis passed.

Other aspects of Jackson's presidency, including his Indian removal policy and his land policies, were given scant treatment by the New Historians, and parts of the interpretation came under considerable revision. In 1932 Thomas Perkins Abernethy, a former student of Turner's, published *From Frontier to Plantation in Tennessee,* the product of diligent study into the politics of which Jackson was a leading figure. Abernethy saw Jackson not as the champion of the common man in a frontier democracy but as a backwoods nabob who opposed democratic movements in his own state, an opportunist and a demagogue who employed democratic cant to satisfy his selfish ends.

That set the stage for the debut of Arthur Schlesinger, Jr., an ardent supporter of Franklin Roosevelt's New Deal (as he understood it). In *The Age of Jackson* (1945) Schlesinger, Jr., reinterpreted the period not as a manifestation of frontier democracy but as the product of eastern, urban, working-class, and intellectual reformers and as the precursor of the New Deal. Schlesinger's work won popular acclaim and a good deal of acceptance by historians. Three years later Richard Hofstadter, another urban easterner but a social democrat, not a liberal, went further in the same direction in *The American Political Tradition.* Jacksonianism was eastern, urban, and class based, Hofstadter agreed, but the typical Jacksonian, far from being anticapitalist, was "an expectant capitalist." Hofstadter wrote that the movement "grew out of expanding opportunities and a common desire to enlarge these opportunities still further by removing restrictions and privileges that had their origin in acts of government; thus, with some qualifications, it was essentially a movement of laissez-faire."[32]

The New Historians were not especially interested in the two decades after Jackson left the White House, except as events con-

32. Arthur M. Schlesinger, Jr., "Richard Hofstadter," in *Pastmasters,* 289.

tributed or seemed to contribute to the widening differences between the sections that culminated in the Civil War. Formulating the standard interpretation of the Civil War was, once again, Charles A. Beard. In 1927 Beard and his wife Mary coauthored *The Rise of American Civilization*, which became an immensely popular textbook. In it, they depicted the Civil War as a "Second American Revolution." The war was an inevitable conflict, they wrote, a "social cataclysm in which the capitalists, laborers, and farmers of the North and West drove from power in the national government the planting aristocracy of the South." Taking the broad view, they added that in "the light of universal history, the fighting was a fleeting incident; the social revolution was the essential portentous outcome." Moreover, while the Union victory destroyed the economic foundation of the South, it "assured the triumph of business enterprise" because of the enormous profits northern businessmen reaped from the war. "When the long military struggle came to an end they had accumulated huge masses of capital and were ready to march resolutely forward to the conquest of the continent." For twenty years and more the Beards' interpretation of the nature and results of the Civil War was predominant.[33]

From a variety of sources, however, an alternative account arose and gained adherents. This was the "repressible conflict" school of Civil War historiography. As for Reconstruction, the period was almost uniformly described as calamitous.[34]

Knowing the tale this far, the reader will not be at a loss to anticipate how the New History treated the closing years of the nineteenth

33. *The Rise of American Civilization* was a two-volume work. The quotations are in McDonald, Decker, and Govan, *Last Best Hope*, 534.

34. McDonald, Decker, and Govan, *Last Best Hope*, 536. An influential "Revisionist" work was Avery Craven's *The Repressible Conflict* (1939), the idea for which had been suggested by Craven's mentor Frederick Jackson Turner. James G. Randall developed the idea in an article entitled "The Blundering Generation" and a pair of books. Other writers followed suit.

century: as a period of unmitigated greed on an unprecedented scale and corruption of a magnitude unparalleled in American history. The Beards told the story in their textbook, but just as popular were the works of the journalist Matthew Josephson, a disciple of Beard's though not his student. Josephson's books were *The Robber Barons* (1934) and *The Politicos, 1865–1896* (1938). The robber barons— "the malefactors of great wealth"—included John D. Rockefeller, Cornelius Vanderbilt, Jay Gould, Jim Fisk, Andrew Carnegie, and hosts of similar types. They rammed through Congress high tariffs, and they bamboozled Congress into granting enormous subsidies of public lands to finance railroad construction. And when the railway system was complete, they bled farmers white in freight charges. ("It costs a bushel of wheat to ship a bushel of wheat.")

The politicos were the vilest predators that ever infested the public councils. Scandals erupted during the Grant administration, and successive presidencies were not much better. Elections at all levels were travesties. The nearest to a decent president was Grover Cleveland, an old-line Jeffersonian Democrat, who was merely ineffective.

Farmers everywhere, who remained a majority of the voting population, fought for reforms, but in vain. As depicted in John D. Hicks's *Populist Revolt,* the farmers led the Greenback Movement, the Granger Movement, and, in the early 1890s, the Populist Movement. The last of these was forward-looking, advocating policies that were ultimately enacted during the New Deal. In 1896 the Populist Party fused with the Democratic Party, whose candidate William Jennings Bryan stirred the country with his Cross of Gold speech ("You shall not press down upon the brow of labor this crown of thorns, you shall not crucify mankind upon a cross of gold"). They lost anyway. Labor fared no better than the farmers; when Coxey's Army marched on Washington, soldiers and police crushed it.

To compound the nation's woes, hordes of immigrants thronged into northern cities, and redeemer governments in the South systematically deprived blacks of their rights. And, oh yes, there was a war. The Spanish-American War resulted not from the sinking of the *Maine* or similar Spanish misdeeds but in response to a combination of American do-goodism (uplifting the heathen) and jingoistic, capitalistic imperialism. Or so wrote Julius Pratt in *Expansionists of 1898* (1936).

All told, it was not a pretty time.

But the good guys were about to gallop to the rescue in the Progressive Movement. Between 1900 and 1917, reformers from New York to California gained control of state legislatures and governorships, despite fierce opposition from urban machine politicians and business interests, and enacted a huge list of corrective measures. These heroes included Charles Evans Hughes, Frank O. Lowden, George W. Norris, William E. Borah, Hiram Johnson, and the archetype of the successful progressive, Robert M. La Follette of Wisconsin. Under La Follette's leadership, his state adopted "the Wisconsin Idea," whereby the university became the brains of the state government, and the campus's boundaries became the state's boundaries.

The Progressive Movement burst upon the national scene in September 1901 when Vice President Theodore Roosevelt succeeded to the presidency. He brought to the office unprecedented vigor; he was an impressive trust-buster, a tamer of big business, and a keen conservationist. His activities were given considerable impetus by reform journalists known as muckrakers. Their works, together with a muckraking novel by Upton Sinclair called *The Jungle,* led to the passage in 1906 of the Pure Food and Drug Act and the Meat Inspection Act, the latter supposedly over the bitter opposition of the Big Six meatpacking companies.

In the conduct of foreign relations, Roosevelt was equally vigorous. His aim was to build American power and gain the respect of the world. Toward that end he oversaw the expansion of the navy and participated in international conferences. His biggest triumph was the covert sponsorship of Panama's independence from Colombia and the subsequent leasing of the right to dig the Panama Canal. Quite as important, at least for a time, was the Roosevelt Corollary to the Monroe Doctrine, under which American armed forces were in and out of Santo Domingo, Haiti, Nicaragua, Honduras, Mexico, and other nations for twenty-eight years.

Roosevelt was followed by the unfortunate William Howard Taft. Taft was enormously fat and had the personality of a dead halibut, and after the glamorous reign of Roosevelt he was without influence. The economy again struggled in the wake of the Panic of 1907. Nor did it help that rebellion arose in the ranks of Progressives. Convinced that Taft had sold out to the "Interests," Roosevelt made a bid for a third term in 1912. Failing to win the Republican nomination, he ran as a third-party candidate, splitting the Republican vote and putting the Democrat Woodrow Wilson in the White House.

Wilson was idolized by the New Historians; after all, he was a historian. The reforms enacted during his administration were far-reaching, and unlike his predecessors, he was personally responsible for the legislation. He greatly admired the parliamentary system of government and strove to make the American government equally efficient. He resumed the practice (abandoned since Jefferson) of appearing in person before Congress as if he were a prime minister, and he not only presented legislation but also worked actively to bring about its passage.

The era of progressive reform ended abruptly and tragically upon America's entry into World War I. In the 1930s the Nye Committee revealed sensational charges that munitions makers and bankers had maneuvered the country into war. Beard wrote a book, *The Devil Theory of War* (1935), essentially endorsing that view. Most New Historians were unwilling to go that far. What they did agree was that the Senate, by blocking ratification of the Treaty of Versailles and thus keeping the United States out of Wilson's cherished League of Nations, had killed a grand opportunity for making the world safe for democracy.

The New Historians' depiction of the 1920s can be summarized briefly. When I was a student, the chapter on the twenties in virtually every textbook was headed, "Isolationism and Reaction." As for isolationism, the United States turned its back on Europe and on its responsibilities in Latin America. "Reaction" indicated that Americans were sick unto death of crusades, domestic or foreign, and wanted only to enjoy themselves in a return to "normalcy." That return entailed corruption on a scale not seen since the days of Grant. Fortunately for President Warren G. Harding, he died. His successor, Calvin Coolidge, was a narrow man, given to inane utterances: "the business of America is business"; "the principal ideal of the American people is idealism." When he was running for election in 1924, the voters (who now included women) were urged to "keep cool with Coolidge." They ate it up, and he won by a landslide despite the candidacy as a Progressive of the old warhorse La Follette.

The business of America was a sordid affair. Perhaps the worst offenders were the lords of electric utility holding companies, who invented a pyramid form of acquiring operating companies, whereby a million dollars invested at the top could control a hundred million dollars' worth of tangible property. When the inevitable stock market crash came, the high fliers took the dive. The Hoover administration did nothing, and the depression deepened steadily.

Coverage of the New Deal can also be treated briefly. Indeed, the New Deal was not history during the heyday of the New Historians; it was current events. Nonetheless, the historians had their attitudes about what Roosevelt's place in history would be: overwhelmingly they saw him as an inspiring leader, almost a godlike figure, destined to be remembered as the greatest president. In broad terms, the New Deal was seen as having three goals: relief, recovery, and reform. The multitude of programs and laws directed toward those ends, when coupled with Roosevelt's leadership, saved capitalism from itself and prevented the United States from falling into extremism on the Right, namely, fascism, or extremism on the Left, namely, communism.

As I look back at this tale told by the New Historians, it strikes me as being a caricature: could any intelligent human being believe such a story? I can assure you that they did. The majority of American historians thought of the story as tough-minded, sophisticated, and realistic.

Little did they know—and I mean that literally.

■

THREE

A New Game and a New Player

Beard began his preface to *An Economic Interpretation* with the words, "The following pages are frankly fragmentary." He offered as his reason for not treating the subject fully the explanation that "I am unable to give more than an occasional period to uninterrupted studies, and I cannot expect, therefore, to complete within a reasonable time the survey which I have made here." His avowed purpose in publishing the abbreviated form was to encourage "a few of this generation of historical scholars . . . to turn away from barren 'political' history to a study of the real economic forces which condition great movements in politics."[1]

In his second substantive chapter Beard revealed, perhaps inadvertently, a barrier more formidable than the pressure of time: the necessary primary sources were simply not available when he wrote in 1913. Among the crucial records, for instance, were those showing the distribution of the ownership of Revolutionary War debts.

---

1. Charles A. Beard, *An Economic Interpretation of the Constitution of the United States,* with an introduction by Forrest McDonald (New York, 1986), v.

He was the first scholar to study those records, then lodged in the basement of the Treasury Department. He indicated that he was able to "use some of the records only after a vacuum cleaner had been brought in to excavate the ruins." A number had disappeared forever, for a janitor had "sold a cart-load or more of these records to a junk dealer" (eighteenth-century paper was made of linen rags and therefore had commercial value). Then Beard made an important suggestion: "Unless the Government at Washington follows the example of enlightened administrations in Europe and establishes a Hall of Records, the precious volumes which have come down to us will be worked only with great difficulty, if they do not disintegrate and disappear altogether."[2]

As it happened, the creation of the National Archives was authorized by Congress not long after the publication of the 1935 edition of *An Economic Interpretation,* and this was just one of many changes taking place that were to cause a massive expansion of mineable sources for American history. During the Great Depression the Works Progress Administration, an agency created to put people to work in a variety of menial tasks, also employed thousands of white-collar types to collect and house historical records. Shortly after World War II, state governments, their treasuries temporarily bloated, established state archives, supplementing the work already being done by state and local historical societies. The advent of microfilm made possible a host of record-gathering projects, including collecting the extant newspapers published in America prior to 1820 and collecting the colonial and state government records for the same period. The plethora of source materials readily available by the early 1950s was such that, had Beard had access to them, he could easily have made his work a great deal less fragmentary, even given the restraints on his time.

And sundry restraints on the college professor/historian were

2. Ibid., 22, 22 n.

being dissolved as well. Typically, professors of Beard's generation were required to teach five and six courses per semester on a wide range of subjects. By the late 1950s, despite increases in the number of students, teaching loads in many colleges and universities were falling to three or fewer courses per semester. Emphasis upon research as the key to professional advancement provided the incentive for the enlarged professoriat to exploit the newly convenient resources, the adoption of generous leave policies provided the opportunity, and the expansion of research grants provided the wherewithal. Moreover, travel to state archives and historical societies and the Library of Congress was cheap, as were accommodations near the repositories.

These conditions, which brought about a revolution in the quantity and quality of easily tapped information concerning the American past, lasted about a quarter of a century, during which it was possible for a historian to do more research in a year than could have been done in a lifetime when Beard was a young man. Luckily I entered the profession at the beginning of that halcyon age.

As a child in Orange, Texas (population about 7,500), in the 1930s, I had no aspiration to become a historian. Indeed, I doubt whether I knew such a creature existed. But like most Texas kids of my generation, I had history repeatedly drummed into my consciousness, especially Texas history. I knew that the flags of six nations (Spain, France, Mexico, the Republic of Texas, the United States, and the Confederacy) had flown over Texas. I knew about Stephen F. Austin and Sam Houston and the Alamo and Davy Crockett and Jim Bowie and William Barrett Travis. I knew about Dick Dowling, the sixteen-year-old who had repelled the Union attack at the Battle of Sabine Pass. I knew these things because we were taught them in school and because the Humble Oil and Refining Company (predecessor of Esso and then Exxon) compiled and distributed to every sixth-grader in the state a fat comic book tracing the history of Texas over the 400-plus years after its discovery by Nuñez Cabeza de Vaca in 1528. In addition, I had forebears who had died in the Civil War and uncles who had served in France during World War I, and I could listen endlessly to yarns about those conflicts. In sum, I was steeped in and appreciative of my heritage.

But my true love was baseball, and to become a major league baseball player was my burning ambition from the time I was ten years old. That was rather a strange ambition given the place and time, for my peers were interested only in football: Orange had a baseball park but no little leagues and no high school baseball team. Nonetheless, I devoured the sport on radio and in the newspapers and organized pickup games whenever I could. The closest I came to practicing was with my friend George W. "Tater" Raborn. Tater was a big ox of a fellow who would later become the Southwest Conference shotput champion and whose greatest pleasure in life was to stand at home plate, throw up a ball, and try to hit it over the fence some 320 feet away. I would play the outfield and chase the balls as he hit them. I was fast and well coordinated and could catch nearly everything he hit that fell short of the fence. I also had an arm like a rifle. I believed, and believe to this day, that as an outfielder I was of major league caliber.

The logical thing, upon graduating from high school, was for me to go to the University of Texas to participate in its highly rated baseball program. I went to the university solely to play baseball. Alas, it turned out that I was "good field, no hit," or, more specifically, that I could not hit a curve ball for the life of me.

I rarely attended classes—after a year I was still a second-semester freshman—but curiously, I was unconsciously preparing myself to become a historian. During the off-season, I spent countless hours in the university's newspaper collection reading about baseball. I read the entire file of the *New York Times* from 1900 to 1944, summers only, sports pages only: I read the *Times'* account of every major league game during that period. Much later I realized that I had been doing historical research and had become a veritable encyclopedia of the history of the sport.

Then I joined the navy to avoid being drafted into the army, and during my year and a half in service I was smitten by another burning ambition. Discarding the childish dream of becoming a ballplayer, I settled upon the more realistic dream of writing the great American novel. Except when in combat, service people have lots of time on their hands, even during a war—the adage "hurry up and wait" describes the life—and consequently I and many of my mates read a lot. What was available on bases and shipboard was mainly junk, and we devoured it. I enjoyed the humorous writings of H. Allen Smith, read and reread James T. Farrell's *Studs Lonigan Trilogy* (which would become relevant to my life as a historian), and was particularly taken with the novels of James M. Cain, a successful writer in the "hard-boiled" school of sex and violence. He wrote *Double Indemnity, Mildred Pierce,* and *The Postman Always Rings Twice,* each of which was made into a hit movie.

I decided I could write like Cain—but better—and set out to do so. As it happened, toward the end of my hitch in the navy I was the sole aviation radioman on a blimp base, and I had a building all to myself. The building contained a typewriter, and I banged out my first (and last) novel before being discharged. It was immature and was never published, but the experience of writing it taught me what to do next: return to the university and take a degree in English, which would prepare me for my career as a novelist. Accordingly, I reentered the University of Texas in January 1947, shortly after my twentieth birthday.

I had a couple of special gifts going for me: boundless self-confidence and inexhaustible energy. The normal course load for undergraduates was fifteen hours, five courses a semester; I took six and seven courses and augmented them by occasional correspondence courses. As a result, I went from second-semester freshman to a master's degree in two years and eight months. Moreover, though

In the navy, 1945; Forrest flanked by Howie McAvoy (*left*) and P. R.
Lund (*right*)

I was partially supported by the G.I. Bill of Rights for a portion of the time, I found it necessary to work at an assortment of jobs to support myself and my growing family—a wife and two children, in time to become five. My mainstay position was as a janitor for the University Press, then just a printing plant, at which I worked thirty hours a week, but I supplemented my $19.12 weekly paycheck by moonlighting at various jobs. For some time I worked with my younger brother Jim (who had a football scholarship and in his senior year became a team captain) in delivering the campus newspaper, the *Daily Texan*. Though Jim went on to become a successful lawyer, we agree that we were more adept at delivering newspapers than at any other endeavor. We had four routes covering twenty miles and totaling 1,600 papers, and we consistently delivered them in under fifty minutes, our record being forty-one minutes. Nor were the papers the small sheets one thinks of as typical college newspapers; they were full sized and ran as many as eighty pages.

Thus, while I was whizzing through college I was working on average forty hours a week. At one point, in my last semester of classes, I took six courses (all A's) and worked sixty-six hours a week. For several years I got by on four and a half hours of sleep per night, except on Saturday nights, when I skipped sleep entirely in order to study.

Along the way I decided to forgo my career as a novelist and become a historian instead. The decision came in a rush. I took a junior-level history course under Dr. Barker that was supposed to cover the United States from the Revolution to the election of Jackson but actually consisted of a running denunciation of Beard's *Economic Interpretation*. Knowing nothing of the subject, I dutifully recorded the lectures in my notebook and accepted Barker's pronouncements as gospel. The next semester I took a course in government under a budding hotshot named H. Malcolm Macdonald that was entitled "Twentieth-Century Political Thought" but covered political thinkers from John Locke through Karl Marx. One day, discussing the American Constitution, Macdonald recited Beard's interpretation as if it were his own. After class, I went up to him and said, "Dr. Macdonald, that is what Charles A. Beard says about the Constitution." Macdonald replied, "That's right." I stammered, "But, but, Dr. Barker says that Beard is all wrong." Macdonald looked me straight in the eye and said, "Eugene Campbell Barker is a senile old man." Stunned, I brooded on the matter and then thought to myself that if learned scholars could disagree about as fundamental a subject as the formation of the United States Constitution, the field of American history must be absolutely wide open.

That was in the fall of 1948; the following January I called on Barker in his office and told him I would like to write a master's thesis on Beard's economic interpretation, and asked if he would direct it. What part of Beard's interpretation, he wanted to know. "All of it," I said. I learned later that he was amused at my presumptuousness—he had a student just then completing a huge doctoral dissertation on ratification in North Carolina alone—but he agreed to let me try. I plunged into the research at a demonic pace, capping my study by hitchhiking from Austin to Washington and back in a week, spending my time in Washington at the National Archives, poring through the Treasury Department records whose use Beard had pioneered. The thesis was finished and accepted in August. It ran to 272 pages, and in retrospect it is stunningly puerile, but it impressed Barker and the other readers as a tour de force.

My mentors encouraged me to pursue a doctorate and to apply for a grant from the Washington-based Social Science Research Council. To my amazement, the council voted to award me a Research Training Fellowship. The standard stipend was $2,500, but inasmuch as I had proposed in my application to spend the fellowship year doing research at repositories from Georgia to New Hampshire, another $1,500 was thrown in as a travel allowance. The total of $4,000 was beyond my wildest dreams; to appreciate how much money it was in 1950, consider that Walter Prescott

Webb, the university's most renowned historian, earned a salary of $6,000, and the legislatively mandated ceiling on professorial salaries was $7,200.

I spent the 1949–1950 academic year completing my course work. I had as yet neither fulfilled my language requirements nor passed my written and oral preliminary examinations, but I figured to knock those off in due course. Then, come the fall of 1950, I would be up and running.

But not so fast, for just then Fulmer Mood entered my life. Barker retired in 1950 and, on the recommendation of Mood's intimate friend Merle Curti, Mood was engaged to replace him. Mood was an eccentric and could afford to be one because he had inherited substantial property. He had a nationwide reputation and gifts that considerably exceeded his accomplishments. He had been a student of Frederick Jackson Turner at Harvard, was generally regarded as the foremost expert on Turner and his works, and had been anointed as the biographer of Turner by the small army of Turner's disciples. He had held a variety of administrative and teaching positions, the most recent being a temporary slot at Wisconsin.

Fulmer and I inherited one another, so to speak; I became his personal research assistant as well as a teaching fellow, which influenced me to follow his advice and wait until the next June before setting out on my research jaunt. His motive, I realized later, was to train me to be something a bit more than a talented but extremely callow youth. He wisely counseled me to change entirely my approach to the study of the origins of the Constitution. One cannot understand an event of 1787–1788 by starting in 1787–1788, he said. You must start at least as far back as 1776, and probably as early as 1763. (I ultimately came to understand that one had to start in ancient times, but that was far in the future.)

Toward the end of reorienting my approach to history, he put me to work on an assortment of tasks. He had me read and take notes on every statute enacted by the British Parliament between 1763 and 1783. He had me do the same with the statutes of each of the thirteen colonies/states. He had me read and record the votes, by members, of every state legislative session from 1781 to 1790. By the time I was ready for the road in June of 1951, I was considerably better prepared than I had been the previous September.

I must pause a bit here to illustrate what kind of time, place, and profession I was entering. During the summer of 1950 I had to prepare to take my oral exams in the fall and needed to take a break from my jobs. I could not afford to, so Walter Webb accompanied me to a bank and personally cosigned a note for $500, which saw me through. I was able to pay most of that off by the following spring, but I was still deep in debt and needed to buy a good used car. Fulmer called upon Mr. Lem Scarborough, owner of the largest department store in Austin, explained my circumstances, and assured him that I was going to be a credit to the university and the state of Texas; whereupon Mr. Scarborough made a $1,000 contribution to the university to establish a one-time-only scholarship to be awarded to someone who exactly fit my description. Professors took care of their students in those days.

I set forth in June of 1951, first depositing my wife and two wee ones with my parents in Orange, and drove to Atlanta in my 1946 Plymouth. Fulmer and I had an understanding as to how I should proceed: I would track down every records repository from Georgia to New Hampshire and make full notes of anything I could find pertaining to the political, economic, social, constitutional, and legal developments, state by state, from the Revolution to 1790. I was to write him a long letter once a week, telling him of my findings and what I thought about them. His theory was that as I went along I would be bristling with ideas that I would be likely to forget when I moved to the next place. He would (and did) return the letters to me when my research travels ended.

In Atlanta, my first stop, I received a welcome that proved to be typical. The state Department of Archives and History had just opened in a house on Peachtree Street, and the manuscript records were literally stacked in piles on the floor. The people in charge greeted me warmly: here was an honest-to-God historian come to study their records. Never mind that I was a fuzzy-cheeked twenty-four-year-old kid who looked seventeen; I was a bona fide historian, and they were thrilled. The same kind of welcome was forthcoming at my next stop, the Georgia Historical Society in Savannah, where Mrs. Mary Bryan, who knew the records backward and forward and was accustomed to dealing with elderly antiquarians, generously and carefully showed me through the materials and pointed out many things I might have missed.

Heading next for South Carolina, I stumbled into a gold mine. The Charleston Library Society had a collection of newspapers for my period that had never been microfilmed and, as far as I could ascertain, had never been used by a historian. Moreover, Charleston during the 1780s had two daily newspapers—papers were mostly weeklies elsewhere—and among their treasures were accounts of debates in the state legislature. The Library Society was a private organization, but a nonmember could use its sources for a fee of fifty cents a day. Inasmuch as I was able to rent a room in a boardinghouse for a dollar a day, the fee was not as trivial as it may sound.

I was treated respectfully there, for Charlestonians are hospitable people, but the touch of awe that had greeted me in Georgia was absent, and for a good reason. Not long before, Allan Nevins had stopped in Charleston and in Columbia with his assistants. When I learned that a week was the total amount of time he had spent in the state doing research for his monumental six-volume Civil War opus, I was bewildered. That seemed an entirely inadequate amount of research, inasmuch as South Carolina had been rather pivotal to the secession movement that led to the war. I remember thinking, I am spending weeks on a less complex period, and nobody can be that much better than I am. Subsequently, however, I learned from his graduate students that Nevins had a truly formidable brain, a gift for reading at superfast speed, and a photographic memory, and I decided that maybe he was that much better.

From Charleston I went to Columbia, where the director of the South Carolina Archives was a former classmate of Fulmer's, Dr. J. Harold Easterby. The material there was more easily usable than the records in Georgia, having been systematically arranged, bound, and in some instances catalogued. Of particular value were records of state finances and imports and exports during the period; these were matters that Beard had overlooked and that Charles G. Singer, the author of the only monograph about South Carolina during the Confederation, had treated inadequately.

North Carolina proved to be a special case. On the one hand, the state had been the subject of good monographs and articles concerning the period, including the doctoral dissertation by Dr. Barker's student William Clay Pool, and thus less original work on my part was necessary. On the other, a pivotal question regarding North Carolina appeared to be unanswerable. North Carolina was dependent upon trade with the outside world, but given its coastline, direct trade was difficult. The normal pattern was for locals to ship their tobacco and naval stores in small crafts to Charleston or Norfolk, whence the goods were transshipped in larger vessels to the West Indies and Europe. The subject had been treated in a doctoral dissertation written by the director of the state records office, Christopher C. Crittenden, titled *The Commerce of North Carolina, 1763–1789,* but Crittenden had not had access to enough records to do a thorough job. I decided that I would piece together the history of North Carolina's trade patterns from shipping records in the neighboring states, which proved to be feasible.

At that point I doubled back to Texas to pick up the family and relocate in the Washington area, planning to do my research on the Middle States from a central base. I could afford to rent a house in Silver Spring, Maryland, for it had a basement apartment that I sublet for two-thirds of what I was paying for the whole house. From there, I worked the Virginia State Library and Virginia Historical Society in Richmond, the Maryland Hall of Records in Annapolis, and, above all, the National Archives and the Manuscripts Division of the Library of Congress.

Rather than describe what I found in those rich repositories, I may mention something of the conditions under which I worked. When doing research in Richmond, I left home early on Monday morning and, after a drive of two hours, arrived at the library when it opened at eight. The library had invaluable records: the Naval Officer Returns (containing full import and export data for each of the state's ports) and the real and personal property records for every county in the state from 1780 onward. Librarians brought out as many of the volumes as I requested, and I sat there for twelve hours at a crack taking notes. Then I went to a nearby Italian restaurant where a large plate of spaghetti and meatballs cost seventy-five cents. After eating I drove out to an abandoned field north of town and spent the night in my car; next day I cleaned up at a truck stop and then repeated my day's work at the library. Afterwards I drove home to Silver Spring. Wednesdays I worked the Archives or Library of Congress. Thursday and Friday were a replay of Monday and Tuesday. That way I got in forty-eight hours of research in Richmond, plus that in Washington, and spent less than four dollars over and above the price of gasoline.

In the National Archives I worked mainly with the Records of the Loan of 1790, the funding of the Revolutionary War debts. I was given full rein to wander in the stacks, absolutely uninterrupted, and when the stacks closed (at five o'clock, I think) I could have volumes moved to the public reading room, which remained open until nine. I was able to examine and take notes on thousands and thousands of transactions, recorded in more than a thousand volumes.

By this time I had gone far beyond aiming for a book about the Beard thesis, and Fulmer and I had decided upon a grand project. I proposed to write perhaps a three-volume work essentially retracing the territory that Allan Nevins had covered in his pioneering (1924) work *The American States during and after the Revolution,* capping it with an account of the writing and ratification of the Constitution.

That decision necessitated research in the northern states at least as intensive as what I had done for the southern, and it entailed changed living arrangements as well. I could scarcely traipse around for months on end with my family in Maryland, so I moved them back to Texas—this time to Austin, where they could live in low-rent university housing while I was away. In Austin I conferred with Fulmer, who had arranged a windfall for me. He had an old friend named Harland Manchester who was a highly successful freelance writer in New York. Harland had an apartment in Greenwich Village where he lived with his wife and two children, and he had a modest (rent-controlled) apartment in the building next door that he used for an office. Fulmer, knowing that I would have to spend a great deal of time in New York, which I could scarcely afford, asked Harland to let me use the office for living quarters when I was in the city. Harland generously agreed, and indeed for two decades I had a free place to live whenever I was in New York.

I set out again in December 1951, stopping in New York for the annual meeting of the American Historical Association before pushing on to Concord, New Hampshire. In New England I found a trove of previously unmined sources that made those in the South seem scanty. The quantity did not surprise me, for I knew that Yankees had long been intensely aware and proud of their history. What did surprise me was the extent to which they had been town oriented and the availability of town-meeting records. I pored over these enthusiastically and went through conventional state sources as well.

Along the way I encountered two senior historians who influenced my future considerably. The first was James B. Hedges of Brown University. Hedges, a former student of Turner's and colleague of Fulmer's, had started as a historian of the West, and he had

had the insight that the trans-Mississippi railroads, upon gaining title to millions of acres of federal lands as a subsidy, were primarily real estate vendors and only secondarily transportation companies. His work and that of his students set off a revolution in the study both of the West and of the railroad business.

In recent years Hedges had acquired access to the collection of papers of the Brown family of Providence, who had become wealthy merchants before the Revolution and continued to be dynamic entrepreneurs well into the twentieth century. Thenceforth he made the Brown family history his life's work. At the time I met him he was in the middle of the research for his first volume, which made him extremely well versed in the period on which I was working. He generously shared information with me, and somehow I managed to impress him, too.

The second was Roy Franklin Nichols, a towering figure among historians of American politics who taught at the University of Pennsylvania. Nichols was a member of the governing board of the Social Science Research Council, in which role he read the quarterly progress reports that we Research Training Fellows were required to submit. He had a special interest in my reports because two of his graduate students, Richard P. McCormick and John A. Munroe, had recently published dissertations on New Jersey and Delaware, respectively, that covered the Confederation period. He was apparently impressed, partly because what I was finding was compatible with what McCormick and Munroe had found and at variance with the conventional accounts of the period. In any event, he sought me out, and we talked briefly at the December convention and arranged for me to spend time with him when I got to Philadelphia. What was crucially important was that somehow—if I ever knew how, I have forgotten—the council decided to renew my fellowship for another year. The renewal was all but unprecedented, and it gave me the opportunity to retrace my footsteps and double the depth of my research.

I shan't recapitulate my further researches here, but merely summarize them. When the work was completed I had compiled more than 5,000 pages of notes, every one crammed full. Historians of a previous generation could not have amassed that quantity of material in many years. I have drawn on those notes for half a century and could still milk them for another dozen monographs.

Meanwhile, the time had come to hunt for a job. The expectation was, if one was getting a Ph.D. in history, that one intended to make a career as a college professor, but the market for history professors had disappeared. The postwar boom in college enrollments, fed by the returning veterans, had collapsed, and the number of Ph.D.s had swollen enormously. Competition for positions was keen, and the pickings were slim. Two of my friends who entered the job market in 1953, both highly competent young historians, illustrate the problem: Peter Coleman landed a job at the University of Manitoba at the magnificent salary of $2,800 a year and a teaching load of six courses per semester; Ray Ginger found a spot at Western Reserve for $3,000 a year. My teaching prospects included a one-year fill-in job at Amherst and a three-year appointment at Ohio State with no possibility of tenure. (For the benefit of the uninitiated, tenure was a standing, hard won by the American Association of University Professors and similar organizations, whereby after a few years a teacher could earn lifetime employment security, revokable only for moral turpitude or incompetence, neither of which was easy to demonstrate; in recent years budgetary stringency has made tenure less absolute.)

Once again Fulmer rescued me. He had sung my praises among the historians in Madison, both at the University of Wisconsin and at the State Historical Society, and though there was nothing doing at the university, Clifford Lord, the director of the Historical Society, showed an interest. Fulmer introduced us at the December 1952 meeting of the American Historical Association, and Lord offered me a job beginning the following June. He had, he said, been nego-tiating with the trade association for the paper industry in Wiscon-sin and with the Wisconsin Utilities Association for a subsidy to hire someone to write a history of the paper business or the electric power industry, and was confident the negotiations would soon bear fruit. He thought the paper people were more likely to come through, but he would give me whichever came first. If neither ma-terialized by June, he would put me to work doing something. My salary was to be $4,000 a year for up to three years, plus a $2,000 annual travel allowance. Knowing nothing whatever about either the business of manufacturing and marketing paper or electric util-ities, I nonetheless snapped up the offer.

The project turned out to be the history of the electric utilities. The arrangement was that the Wisconsin Utilities Association made a grant to the Historical Society large enough to cover my salary and expenses as well as overhead. I would be employed by the Histori-cal Society, not the association or its member companies. Each com-pany would appoint a delegate to a history committee who would act as my liaison with his company's records, which were to be made available to me without reservation, and would arrange any inter-views I requested. When the history was written, each member of the committee would read the manuscript and offer criticisms or suggestions. The contract specifically stated that in case of dis-agreement about facts or interpretations, we would review the records together, but that I alone would have the final say as to how the manuscript would read.

The arrangement was comfortable, and I plunged into the re-search with as much enthusiasm as I had recently devoted to the eighteenth century. I got off to a good start with the committee, de-spite my total ignorance of the subject. At our first meeting, every member except one was present, and someone said that the only his-tory in which the absentee was interested was the history of baseball and cracked, "if you wanted to talk about who led the American

League in batting in 1911, he would sit up and take notice." I replied immediately, "Ty Cobb led the league with a .420 average. Shoeless Joe Jackson was second with a .408 average." I may not have known electricity, but I did know baseball.

A further help was that I turned out to have a hitherto unsuspected talent. I have a natural gift for understanding complex financial affairs. I never had a course in finance or economics, and as a student I had shown no interest in the subject. But when I came to study the extremely complex public finances of the Confederation period, it was easy as pie for me, and the same turned out to be true for the intricacies of public utility finance.

Before tackling any company records, I had to familiarize myself with the evolution of electrical technology and with electric utility economics. The effort had a potent effect on my future work. For the technology part, I read the files of *Popular Science* for the last quarter of the nineteenth century and the first quarter of the twentieth. For the economics, I stumbled upon two volumes of speeches of Samuel Insull, who had been the pioneer in working them out. I had known little about Insull. I remembered vaguely that the collapse in 1932 had been "the biggest business failure in the history of the world," and I recalled Studs Lonigan's agonizing over the impending failure of a Chicago tycoon named Ingersoll. I now came to realize how important Insull was to my project, and I longed to study his personal and corporate records and to write his biography. When I learned that his son was alive and running an insurance business in Chicago, I wrote to him, sought and received an interview, and began to connive to gain access to the necessary documents.

During my first year in Wisconsin my optimistic disposition received a minor jolt. Fulmer had warned me before I left Austin to keep my research and my ideas close to my chest, even in writing my grant reports, for, he said, the history profession was infested by thieves who would steal your material given half a chance. He told me that when he was working on his dissertation, he had gathered a great deal of research notes in Europe and had entrusted them to his dissertation director, Samuel Eliot Morison, who gutted the materials and published an article based on them. I had no reason to question his statement, but being of a trusting nature, I did not take his warning seriously and thought it rather silly.

I soon learned otherwise. In Wisconsin my next-door neighbor was a Presbyterian minister, and I regularly attended his church. One morning he preached a sermon regarding religion and the framing of the Constitution. I did not think he was on sound ground, and I afterward asked him where he got his information. He showed me an article by someone of whom I had never heard, and when I looked at the footnotes I saw a reference to a historian of American religion named William Warren Sweet. It happened that Sweet had taught a two-semester seminar as a visiting professor at the University of Texas a few years before, and I had taken his course. I wrote a paper on religious bodies and the ratification of the Constitution and got an A on it. A year later I asked Sweet for a recommendation, but he seemingly did not remember me and asked what grade I had made. When I said an A, he was skeptical and brushed me aside. Now I went into the library and, taking out his book, found a chapter entitled, "Religious Bodies and the Ratification of the Constitution." It was my paper, verbatim, presented as his own with no mention of me. I did nothing about it, because subsequent research had convinced me that my paper was full of holes. The episode suggested to me, however, that maybe Fulmer was right.

Had I known what I had stumbled into in Wisconsin, I might have been considerably more wary. The political ambience in Madison was extremely left wing. Curti had apparently been a communist (as had Fulmer) until he, like most American communists, was repelled by the 1939 Hitler-Stalin Pact, and the lot of them were entirely intolerant of contrary opinions. I was not yet the archconservative that I would become; indeed, I had voted for Harry Truman in 1948 and

Adlai Stevenson in 1952. But I was suspect in the eyes of the Wisconsin crowd. For openers, they distrusted southerners, and though we Texans did not regard ourselves as southern, they did. Again, I was on friendly terms with the electric utility industry, which was bête noire to them; they habitually called the industry the "power trust" and suspected it of being behind Senator Joseph McCarthy and similar evils. Most tellingly, they were devout Beardians, fondly referring to him as Uncle Charlie, and unbeknownst to me, Fulmer had repeatedly twitted them by boasting that my work would destroy Beard. I had, of course, abandoned that intention some time ago.

Then happenstance intervened. Fulmer discussed my career outlook with Clifford Lord, and they concluded that it was important for me to finish my degree by sandwiching in, between my research trips for the utility project, a dissertation on an eighteenth-century topic. Fulmer asked, "Is there a dissertation subject you could write up by skimming the material off the top of your notes?" I said, "Sure, I could do the Beard thing." And that is how *We the People* came to pass.

When asked about why I wrote it, however, I have offered a different explanation. I have told the story of something that happened when I was an undergraduate at the University of Texas. The Southwest Conference Track and Field Championship meet was coming up, and the Texas Aggies—the hated Aggies—had lost a couple of their star men due to injuries. The Aggie coach had no recourse but to have the remaining members of his team double up, and one particular Aggie, who had all the endurance in the world, was entered in about eight events.

As the day proceeded, this Aggie was bombing around the field, running the high hurdles, throwing the discus, pole vaulting, broadjumping, and doing well in every event. He was scheduled to participate in the shot put, for which I was acting as a minor official—the guy who sticks the little pin in the ground to mark the farthest put of each contestant. The way the shot put works, each contestant is allowed five throws in a preliminary round, and the top five, as judged by the longest single throw in that round, get three more turns in the final round. The longest single put, in whatever round it comes, is the winner. Contestants are called in alphabetical order; if they do not answer the call, they have to skip that turn.

When this Aggie's name came up the first time, he missed his turn because he was throwing the discus. The second time he was taking his turn in the pole vault. He missed the third call because he was broad jumping, and the fourth because he was running the high hurdles. On the fifth and last call he finally showed up. Without even taking off his sweat suit, he picked up the shot, swung around in the circle, and gave a gargantuan heave—and the shot sailed out, a good ten feet beyond the longest throw of any other participant.

He turned, glowered at the stunned onlookers, and said, "All right, you sons of bitches. There's something for you to shoot at," and he raced off to take part in yet another contest.

And that's why I wrote *We the People*.

FOUR

■

The Adventures of
We the People

The timing and circumstances of the decision to tackle *An Economic Interpretation* head-on were in most respects auspicious but in some nearly fatal. On the positive side, a trail had been blazed. Robert E. Brown was about to publish his *Charles Beard and the Constitution* (1956), a devastating critique of Beard's methodology, his use of evidence, and his logic, and though a number of reviewers deplored Brown's shrillness, they conceded that he had considerably weakened the plausibility of Beard's work.

Further trailblazing had come through the study of newly available documents. Somewhat earlier, Philip A. Crowl had mined the records in Maryland and published a doctoral dissertation showing that no correlation existed between positions taken from 1785 to 1787 regarding debtor-relief activity and Federalism or anti-Federalism during ratification. William Pool published as journal articles his analysis of the 268 delegates to North Carolina's first ratifying convention, which rejected the Constitution, and the 271 delegates to its second convention, which voted to ratify; Pool reported that North Carolina Federalists and anti-Federalists held approximately the same amounts and kinds of property. In 1953 Robert E. Thomas published in the *Journal of Southern History* similar results from Virginia. And as indicated, Richard McCormick and John Munroe showed that Beard's thesis was, if not entirely wrong, quite irrelevant to what had happened in New Jersey and Delaware.[1]

Additional advantages derived from being in Wisconsin. The State Historical Society had a superb library, and among its collections were a large number of local histories. The technological developments that made the production of inexpensive books possible during the late nineteenth century coincided with the centennials of every manner of place and thing, and enterprising publishers hired hack writers to canvass towns and counties on the eastern seaboard with a view to commissioning subsidized histories. Hundreds of these "mug books"—so called because descendants paid to have their ancestors' mugs included—were ground out, and somehow the State Historical Society of Wisconsin acquired and kept copies of them. These works identified by occupation many of the town fathers, thus enabling me to track down a number of obscure characters.

Also in Madison was a book editor named Livia Appel, by reputation the most skilled editor of scholarly books in the country. She had spent ten years as a book editor at the University of Minnesota Press and ten years as director of the University of Wisconsin Press, and in the 1950s she was approaching retirement as book editor at the Historical Society. I was told that Miss Appel had more than once rescued an unpublishable manuscript written by a member of

1. William C. Pool, "An Economic Interpretation of the Ratification of the Federal Constitution in North Carolina," *North Carolina Historical Review* 27 (1950): 119–141, 289–313, 437–461; Philip A. Crowl, *Maryland during and after the Revolution* (Baltimore, 1943); Richard P. McCormick, *Experiment in Independence* (New Brunswick, N.J., 1950); John A. Munroe, *Federalist Delaware* (Philadelphia, 1954); Robert E. Thomas, "The Virginia Convention of 1788: A Criticism of Beard's *An Economic Interpretation of the Constitution*," *Journal of Southern History* 19 (February 1953): 63–72.

the Wisconsin department of history and transformed it into an important book. William B. Hesseltine, the department's southern historian, grumbled that she could make anybody's writing dull, but that was merely because she took his flamboyant and sometimes careless prose and turned it into respectable English. In any event, we became fast friends, and much of what I know about writing—as well as my standard for what is good writing—I learned from her. She guided me in shaping my dissertation, and she edited the final version that became *We the People*.

The situation in Madison was not, however, entirely harmonious. As I was writing the dissertation I was also finishing the manuscript on the electric utility industry, and the electric book was published first. The book elicited howls of rage from the Madison *Capital Times,* a militant old Progressive newspaper. Suddenly the Historical Society, Clifford Lord, the electric industry, the book, and I were involved in a heated political fracas. Various people moved to cover themselves, and I became the object of maneuvering that, had it been successful, could have destroyed my career even as it was beginning. Somehow, I was able to emerge from it all—as the homely saying goes—smelling like a rose.

Given our decision as to how to put the dissertation together, the manuscript almost wrote itself. Bob Brown had attacked Beard's methodology and logic; I would approach the subject from the opposite end. That is, I would assume for the nonce that Beard's formulation of his thesis and of the proper way to test it was sound, and I would test it by filling in the details of his "frankly fragmentary" analysis. To verify or disprove his interpretation, he suggested, it would be necessary to compile economic (and to some extent political) biographies of all the people directly involved in the writing and ratification of the Constitution. If, on comparison of those who supported and those who opposed the Constitution, the Federalists turned out to be a consolidated economic group of personalty interests and the anti-Federalists were mainly small farmers and debtors, Beard's economic interpretation would be pretty conclusively substantiated. If, on the other hand, such a comparison showed that proponents and opponents of the Constitution held approximately the same quantities of the same descriptions of property, one would have to conclude that another explanation of the formation of the Constitution was required.

The number of men involved was staggering: more than 1,700, including the 55 delegates to the Philadelphia Constitutional Convention and the delegates to the fourteen state ratification conventions (counting North Carolina's two). But I already had data on most of them in my notes. Little further digging was necessary, and much of the supplementary information was in the mug-book local histories.

Organizing the study was a self-evident task. The introductory chapter had to summarize Beard's interpretation and set forth how I intended to proceed. Then came a chapter or chapters on the delegates to the Philadelphia Convention. I wanted to do a pair of chapters, one on the economic interests of the delegates, the second on their behavior in the Convention regarding issues affecting those interests, but Fulmer insisted that I include a third concerning the state political affiliations of the delegates. I made the addition with misgivings, and I still think that it does not really belong.

Next came three chapters concerning ratification that constituted more than half the work and the greater part of its substance. A chapter covered the five states in which little or no opposition to ratification appeared: Delaware, New Jersey, Georgia, Connecticut, and Maryland. Another considered the states that were divided on the question: Pennsylvania, Massachusetts, South Carolina, and New Hampshire. The next included the states in which the opposition was powerful and came within an ace of success. Inside each chapter, I wrote a brief account of the political and economic history of the states during the period, one by one, followed by a short narrative of the process of ratification and the economic biographies of the delegates whose holdings and occupations I could identify.

Then came concluding chapters, the key chapter being number eight, "A Revaluation of the Beard Thesis of the Making of the Constitution." I started by dealing with the delegates to the Philadelphia Convention that had written the Constitution. I found and reported that fully a fourth of the delegates "had voted in their state legislatures for paper-money and/or debtor-relief laws," just the kinds of laws that, according to Beard, "the delegates had convened to prevent." Another fourth had interests that were adversely affected by the Constitution. The most common and important property held by the delegates was not public securities or other personal property but land. Furthermore, the evidence shows decisively that inside the Convention the delegates "behaved as anything but a consolidated economic group."

As for the supposed division between personalty and realty interest groups in the state ratifying conventions, three states voted unanimously to ratify, so no division was evident, even though most of the delegates in the three were farmers who, according to Beard, should have opposed the Constitution. In two states where ratification was challenged, Virginia and North Carolina, the great majority of delegates were planters with minimal personalty interests except in land speculation, and land speculators were divided on the question. In four contested states, agrarian interests were dominant, but sizable numbers of delegates both pro and con held personal property as well. And in four states (Massachusetts, Pennsylvania, New York, and Rhode Island), men having personalty interests dominated the conventions, but they split almost evenly on the question of ratification.

In regard to public security holding as "a very considerable dynamic element, if not the preponderating element, in bringing about the adoption of the new system" (Beard's words), in five states, such holdings were minimal; in three, they were important but equally divided; in two (Massachusetts and Connecticut), most public security owners favored ratification; but in Pennsylvania, South Carolina, and New York, most security holders opposed ratification.

On all counts, then, I showed that Beard's interpretation was incompatible with the facts. I went on to add two chapters, one analyzing the economic interest groups that actually existed at the time—a far greater array of diverse and complex interests than Beard had described—and another called "Economic Interpretation and the Constitution," which I included after I began to think seriously about methodological and theoretical problems in the study of history.

As I used to tell my students, the very idea of economic man, which the New Historians regarded as hard-boiled realism, is in truth simpleminded. It fails to take into account the complicated range of motivations that impel human beings to do what they do. The idea of man as economic animal fails to consider the driving force that the Framers themselves regarded as the most potent among public men, namely, the love of power. It disregards the actuality that in real life one's economic interests are diverse and often contradictory. And it belittles the notion that patriotism, a sense of duty to one's country, can override selfish considerations of economic gain. That patriotism led some Framers to espouse the Constitution despite their economic interests can be abundantly illustrated. Consider, for example, two delegates to the Convention. Nathaniel Gorham, a devout nationalist, was a wealthy Massachusetts merchant who had contracted to buy a huge tract of land in western New York, the purchase being payable in public securities at par value, though before 1789 the securities could be bought on the open market for ten or fifteen cents on the dollar. The creation of the federal government under the Constitution would send the market prices of securities up toward par. That would ruin Gorham, and he knew it, but he championed the Constitution anyway—and lost his shirt. A similar thing happened to the archnationalist Robert

Morris of Philadelphia, who in 1787 was the richest merchant in America and who ended up in debtors' prison.

Little needs to be added about the actual writing process of *We the People*. I began during the winter of 1954–1955 and completed it in time to be awarded my Ph.D. early in August 1955. I wrote the work while wearing a pistol, for I was moonlighting as a night watchman at a research laboratory to pad my income, and the solitude gave me abundant opportunity to think (I still needed next to no sleep and could carry out my daytime tasks without difficulty).

After the defense of thesis—a mere formality—Fulmer took me to call upon two people for career advice. One was Caleb Perry Patterson, recently retired from the university, who years before had studied under Beard at Columbia and had taken a Ph.D. in government as well as a law degree. He had had opportunities to earn a great deal of money as a lawyer but idealistically chose to devote his life to college teaching. His advice was, "Young man, you have shown that you can do things in the practical world. Forget about college teaching and make yourself a career in business." The other was Walter F. McCaleb, who had taken a Ph.D. with a dissertation on the Burr conspiracy under Hermann von Holst at Chicago early in the century. He had embarked upon a college teaching career but due to family circumstances had been forced to leave academia and become a banker. He had had a long, lucrative career in that profession, culminating in the presidency of the Dallas Federal Reserve Bank. What he said to me was, "Young man, you have the opportunity to devote your life to a noble and rewarding profession. Spurn any temptation to go into business. Devote yourself to teaching and scholarship."

As things happened, I was on a career course that was neither of the above. In the early 1950s Cliff Lord had created an arm of the Historical Society called the American History Research Center, whose purpose was to foster research through grants-in-aid and publication in a field that Lord called "localized" history. The idea was that all history is local, in the sense that erstwhile Speaker of the House Tip O'Neill meant when he said that all politics is local, but local history had by and large been abandoned to antiquarians. "Localized" history would place local events in a broader setting or deal on a large scale with institutions that are always local in character, such as the grand jury. The first person in charge of the Center, its "Chief," held the position for a time but did not do much, and when he found a teaching job he moved on. Lord thought I could handle it, and as I was finishing my dissertation and the electric utility history, he offered me the job, though since I was too young to be called chief of anything, I was to have the more modest title of executive secretary. I liked the goals of the Center, it offered a substantial increase in salary, and I accepted.

The Center had a board of directors, consisting of businessmen friends of the Historical Society, and an Advisory Council that passed on the grants and made decisions about publishing monographs. Among the members of the Advisory Council were Roy Nichols, the medical historian Richard H. Shyrock, Thomas Clark of the University of Kentucky, the longtime editor of the *Journal of Southern History* Wendell Stephenson, the southern historian Winfred Binkley, Cornell's western historian Paul Wallace Gates, and Indiana's R. Carlisle Buley (whose book *The Old Northwest* won what Fulmer called the only deserved Pulitzer Prize). The board met twice a year in conjunction with the meetings of the major historical associations, and it was a privilege for me to work with such an array of historians.

Much of the job was devoted to fund-raising. The Center was given a biennial state appropriation of $15,000, which covered my salary and expenses and a bit of overhead but little else. We contemplated spending a few thousand a year in grants—in those days, a summer research grant of a thousand or even a few hundred dollars could enable a promising young scholar to complete a worthwhile

June 1956; Forrest as newly appointed executive secretary of the
American History Research Center

project that otherwise would not be possible—and publishing two or three monographs a year, which for a press run of a thousand copies would cost $3,000 or $4,000 each. I was not much good as a fund-raiser and did not like doing it, but I raised enough to operate on a hand-to-mouth basis.

During the three years that I ran the Center we accomplished a lot. In addition to subsidizing a number of research projects, we published half a dozen high-quality books. The first was *History of Medicine in Chicago* by Thomas Bonner, who went on to have a notable career as a historian and college president. We published a biography of John Wentworth, a Chicago politician and contemporary of Lincoln, written by Don Fehrenbacher, who would later write a masterful Pulitzer Prize–winning study of the Dred Scott case. We did a work on Memphis during the Progressive Era by William D. Miller and a history of the grand jury in America by Richard Younger. For most of these I was both editor and publication manager, in which capacity (as I wrote the jacket blurbs) I came to learn that reviewers parrot the blurbs as often as they actually review the books.

I met the costs of these projects by a variety of devices. I induced the Chicago Medical Society to buy enough copies of Bonner's book to pay for the printing. I sold a half interest in Miller's book to Memphis State University Press. And along the way I scared up grants from interested individuals to pay for T. Harry Williams' research and writing of his biography of Huey Long, to do the same for Bill Miller's biography of "Boss" E. H. Crump of Memphis, and to hire Livia Appel to edit Tom Govan's biography of Nicholas Biddle, cutting it by a third to make it manageable.

While I was working at the Center—actually, I was the Center— three developments occurred that would have a potent impact upon my future. A few weeks after I took my degree, I was privileged to attend a ten-day conference on historiography at the University of Kansas. Present were James C. Malin and twenty-five or thirty young historians, most of whom would attain eminence during the ensuing decades. They included William Appleman Williams, who was to become the guru of the New Left in the 1960s and 1970s; Robert E. Brown; Robert Ferrell, later perhaps the premier historian of American foreign relations; and a host of others. We were in close proximity throughout the conference, for Kansas is hot in August and the campus at the time had only two air-conditioned buildings. We lived in one and held three formal discussions a day in the other. The result was an intense saturation in the theory and practice of history. That experience, together with endless conversations I later had with a theoretical physicist named Harvey Worthington, led me to write the final chapter on historical method in *We the People*. What I learned and was forced to think about has influenced my practice as a historian ever since.[2]

Not long after the conference, I had the good fortune of becoming the biographer of Samuel Insull. Throughout the years people had approached Samuel Insull, Jr., with proposals to write a biography of his father, several wanting to pay him lavishly for the exclusive rights, some wanting him to pay them to do a puff job. He was impressed by my work on the Wisconsin utilities, and the upshot was that Cliff Lord negotiated a contract with him similar to the Historical Society's arrangement with the Wisconsin Utilities Association. Insull, Jr., would contribute to the Center an amount equal to my annual salary (my salary was paid by legislative appropriation; his contribution would help finance the Center's other activities) and would make available his father's records that he possessed and use his influence to make available the records of companies the elder Insull once managed. When the manuscript was complete, he would be able to read it and suggest corrections or changes; I was to have the sole power to determine how the final text should read.

2. Chapter two, discussing the philosophy of the New Historians, is among the ultimate fruits of the Kansas experience.

The next turn of events was an unfortunate estrangement. After the American Historical Association meeting in Chicago in December 1956, Fulmer and I traveled to New York together, each of us having business there. On New Year's Eve we went to a party with Harland and Laetitia Manchester and their two teenagers. When time came to leave, we could not squeeze into one taxi, so Harland and I followed the others. We got into a deep conversation, stopped at a bar for a couple of drinks, and then walked back to the Manchesters' neighborhood. Laetitia had no key to the office apartment where I was staying, so she had bedded Fulmer on the living room couch in their apartment. The next morning, Fulmer was gone. I learned later that he had awakened early with the sudden realization that I was the head of a conspiracy against him.

Fulmer spent the following summer in his native California doing research, and when he returned to Austin in the fall he proclaimed loudly to the dean that Archie Lewis, the chairman of the history department, had engaged graduate students to spy on him in California. Everyone was embarrassed and sought to keep the matter quiet. Fulmer would have no "cover-ups" and insisted that he had been spied upon. The long and short of it was that he was declared to be a paranoid schizophrenic and relieved of his position at the university. I never saw him again, and he never said or wrote another word to me. The single subsequent contact was indirect: he insisted to Cliff Lord that I dedicate *We the People* to him, which I did.

Let There Be Light: The Electric Utility Industry in Wisconsin, 1881–1955 was published by the American History Research Center in 1957. That it was published by the Center and not by the State Historical Society was at the urging of Cliff Lord. He argued that it fit perfectly into the Center's program of promoting localized history, for it treated the subject in its national and international context as well as on the state and local levels. Moreover, it was the first scholarly treatment of the history of the industry—Raymond C.

Miller's fine history of the Detroit Edison Company was in the works—and as such, Lord insisted, it would be a feather in the Center's cap. I readily agreed, and the Utilities Association did not object. Not until later did I suspect that Lord had an ulterior motive, namely, to deflect potential political heat from the Historical Society.

The book was rather woodenly organized into four periods. Each section contained a chapter on the general scene, one on the local scene, and one on the state scene. The earlier chapters were difficult to follow, for they were loaded with details that readers could not possibly hold in their heads or even care about. Overall, however, the book was reasonable well written, thanks in part to the editorial assistance of Leslie Decker, then the editor of the *Wisconsin Magazine of History*.

Light was well received, attracting positive reviews in the various journals to which we sent it. The serious exception was a review by Louis C. Hunter, best known for his history of steamboating, of all things, who reviewed *Light* in the June 1958 issue of the *Mississippi Valley Historical Review,* predecessor of the *Journal of American History*. Hunter treated *Light* fairly, having good things to say about it as well as mildly critical remarks, but the last third of his review questioned the propriety of the arrangements that had brought the book into being. That it had been financed by the Utilities Association and that I had had the cooperation of a committee of the association had been announced up front in my preface, but Hunter was outraged. He closed with the nasty comment that he wondered "how the State Historical Society, in accepting the grant for this study, conceived its scholarly responsibilities in the project and by what means it proposed to protect the public, the author, and its own reputation from the risks manifest in such an undertaking."

Cliff Lord responded in the December 1958 *Review* with a temperate but firm defence of the whole project, defending the Historical Society, me, and the book. He noted that I had been appointed to the project on the recommendation of scholars whose judgment he trusted, that I had been selected in part because I was an outsider and thus untainted by preconceived notions about Wisconsin politics, and that the Utilities Association had explicitly waived control over what the book should say. He added that the book had been published by the Center, not the Historical Society, and that although the Center's books were generally read and approved by two members of its distinguished Advisory Council and an outside expert, because of the potentially controversial nature of this book, three undisclosed "hostile witnesses" from the outside had also read and recommended publication of the manuscript. Lord's reply was solid, principled, and courageous. The problem was that privately he was striking a different stance.

To make clear what happened, I must backtrack a bit. When I finished my dissertation, Fulmer advised me to pick a publisher carefully and drive a hard bargain; the book would be in print for many years and the royalties would be handsome. He did what he could to promote interest in it, touting it among his wide circle of acquaintances, so that it was known about long before it appeared in print. Indeed, no less a publisher than Alfred A. Knopf (whose regal and pompous presence was such that Tom Govan said of him, "There but for the grace of God goes God") made a special trip to Austin to try to persuade Fulmer to let him publish the book.

But Cliff Lord talked me into letting the Center publish *We the People*. Persuading me was not difficult. I was as confident as anybody about the kind of splash it would make, and from that point of view I naively thought it did not matter much who the publisher was. And, dedicated as I was to making the Center successful, I considered it incumbent on myself to contribute toward that end by whatever means I could. Accordingly, I ignored Fulmer's advice and *donated* the manuscript to the Center, waiving royalty rights. I have no idea how much that cost me over the years, for, not owning the rights, I have never seen the sales figures. But at this writing, *We the People* is still in print.

The Center was, however, on shaky financial footing. Somehow the state appropriation had disappeared into the general funds of the Historical Society without being employed toward either my salary or the Center's grant-making and book-publishing endeavors. By the middle of 1957 (after Fulmer broke with me), we were in arrears on our printing bills, and the Center was hard pressed to scare up the money to publish *We the People*. Lord and I discussed the matter a number of times, but then I came up with a wild idea. We had sold an interest in Bill Miller's book; why not sell a piece of *We the People* to a major university press, say, the University of Chicago? Lord agreed, and I went down to Chicago to talk with Roger Shugg, director of the Press.

Shugg expressed an interest and asked me if I could suggest a couple of reputable readers to appraise the manuscript. My replay was not lacking in audacity. The Press had recently launched its History of American Civilization series under the editorship of Daniel Boorstin, and one of the first volumes was Edmund Morgan's *The Birth of the American Republic, 1763–1789*. I had reviewed the book for the *Wisconsin Magazine of History*, and though my respect for Boorstin and Morgan was and remains large, I found a number of flaws and noted them in my review. Both Boorstin and Morgan were miffed. So, in response to Shugg's question, I said, "Sure. Dan Boorstin and Ed Morgan." Though a bit nonplussed, he sent the manuscript to them, and as I expected, both enthusiastically endorsed it. Consequently, the Center sold a half interest in *We the People* to the University of Chicago Press for the handsome sum of $5,000. The arrangement was that the Press would be the publisher and handle the marketing; the Center would hold the copyright and produce the books.

Money problems continued to plague the Center, however, and early in 1958, to make sure we could pay the costs of printing *We the People*, we resorted to a desperate move. With Lord's permission, I discussed the matter with Insull, Jr. The solvency of the Center was of direct concern to him, and he understood that *We the People* would establish my credentials and thereby make my biography of his father more acceptable to the historical fraternity. He offered to advance a loan to the Center, but that seemed imprudent for a variety of reasons, not least because we had no way of assuring him that we could repay the loan. Finally we agreed to sell him the Center's interest in *We the People* for $5,000. The investment was sound, inasmuch as he would receive half the proceeds from the sale of the book over the years. Now the Center had no stake in the book, just its name on the copyright page remaining as evidence that it had any connection with the publication. But at least the Center could continue to function.

My troubles, however, had not ended. The *Capital Times* had begun its tirade against the Historical Society, Lord, the utilities, and me, and its attacks made the snide comment of Louis Hunter seem like praise. Lord was particularly under fire, and despite the public position he would take in the *Mississippi Valley Historical Review,* in private he distanced himself from me in a variety of ways, making it clear that he regarded me as, if not an outright enemy, at least an unwelcome presence.

The climax came in May. The annual meeting of the board (perhaps the entire membership; my recollection is not clear) of the Historical Society was scheduled to convene in Sturgeon Bay, and Lord, without informing me, called a concurrent meeting of the business board of the Center. I happened to have a friend, Nancy Abraham, who worked as a secretary in the managerial offices of the Historical Society, and by chance she typed the letters convening the Center's board. She was mystified, inasmuch as I had not been invited, and she told me of it. I, too, was mystified and sensed immediately that dirty work was afoot.

I telephoned Insull, Jr., and asked whether he had ever heard of an organization's calling a meeting of its governing body without telling the executive secretary. He advised me to attend the meeting without an invitation and said that he would send Abner J. Stilwell as his personal representative. Stilwell was an almost legendary figure, a retired vice president of the Continental Illinois National Bank and Trust Company. He had been the bank's troubleshooter during the Great Depression, when there was nothing but trouble. He was, to coin a phrase, hard as nails and sharp as a tack. I had met him a number of times, and when Insull told me he would be at Sturgeon Bay, I felt that I was in safe hands no matter what Lord intended.

That feeling vanished once the meeting got under way. The session started late in the evening, probably around ten, and at first the members of the Historical Society's board as well as those of the Center were in attendance. Lord and Bill Hesseltine did all the talking, and for a while it was unclear where they were going. Finally, however, it became evident that they were accusing me of embezzling money from the Center. The sale of the rights to *We the People* (which had been exclusively mine until I gave them to the Center) was somehow being twisted into a charge that I was using the proceeds for my own benefit. Stilwell said not a word, and I felt my career and entire future being flushed down the drain. If I were fired for peculation, my life as a historian would be ended, and Lord could take the pressure off himself by making me the heavy.

Ultimately, they went too far. Either Lord or Hesseltine brought up the name of Insull, Jr., personally—he had been mentioned only in passing before—and suggested that he was implicated in my fraudulent activities. Stilwell pounded one hamlike hand upon the table and said, "Just a damned minute!" There was a hush, and then I realized that Stilwell had been listening intently as Lord and Hesseltine laid out the case, and he proceeded to demolish it utterly. By this time the Society's board members had gone to bed, with the indictment of me still ringing in their ears. The Center's board members sat rapt, and they were visibly appalled by what Lord and Hesseltine had tried to do. They rejected out of hand any idea of censuring me and, as I recall, adopted a resolution commending me for having done an excellent job in running the Center.[3]

The next morning I ran into Donald McNeil, the associate director of the Historical Society, and told him what had happened. He had left the meeting early, and his reaction to my news was, "Good God! How is Cliff going to explain that to the board?" I never learned what his explanation was, but the directorship of the State Historical Society of Wisconsin was no longer a viable position for him. Fortuitously, in short order he was offered and accepted a position as dean of continuing education—employees of the Society sneeringly referred to him as "dean of the night school"—at Columbia University, and he was gone.

Then my career began to rocket into orbit. The first stage was an offer of a good teaching job. I had been offered a job a year earlier: Ralph Hidy, chairman of the history department at the Harvard Business School, had invited me to join his department. At the time, I was not interested in making a move, and besides, I would have been the junior member of a department in which I had published more than anyone except Hidy himself. Now I was quite receptive to an offer, and happily, one came. James B. Hedges had earlier written to Fulmer praising my work, and with his permission we had used excerpts on the back of the dust jacket to *We the People*. When the book appeared, I sent him a copy. At just that moment, Brown University was set to hire four promising young historians, and President Barnaby Keeney had asked Hedges to accept a temporary chairmanship to make the appointments. Hedges agreed, and that same day, he sent me a telegram saying, "Are you permanently

3. When I left Madison, the Center was a few thousand dollars in debt. Shortly after I arrived in Providence, I was able to persuade a friend in the foundation business, Kenneth Templeton, to make a grant to Brown equal to the debt, with which it formally purchased the Center and all its rights, including a sizable stock of books that were then transferred to the Brown University Press.

committed to your present type of work? If not, I should like to try to persuade you to accept a position at Brown." I telegraphed back that I was not committed. He then arranged for me to go to Providence and talk with him and Keeney. On the spot, they made me a substantial offer as a tenured associate professor. I accepted on one condition: since I could not move in September, for I had work to finish in Madison, I would begin at Brown in January of 1959. That was agreed to.

The good fortune of having brought the University of Chicago Press into the situation then began to pay off handsomely. Had *We the People* been published by the Center, as originally planned, I would never have thought to send review copies to major outlets such as the *New York Times* or the *Saturday Review,* and they probably would have ignored the book if I had. But Roger Shugg thought big, the University of Chicago Press was a big-time operation, and he sent copies to everybody.

The first dividend appeared in the *Saturday Review* for October 11, 1958, with a review by David M. Potter of Yale. The review began by saying that in "'WE THE PEOPLE' Forrest McDonald has written what may prove to be one of the most important books on American history in recent years. . . . it subjects Charles A. Beard's economic interpretation of the Constitution to one of the most smashing analyses ever mounted in the literature of historical criticism." Midway through the review, warming to the subject, he wrote, "McDonald has done a staggering amount of research— those 'years of research' in the local records which seemed so impossible to Beard and in fact would seem impossible to almost anyone else." And in his concluding paragraph Potter wrote, "Readers who prefer pulse-stirring history will quail at the remorseless detail of McDonald's unrelenting analysis. He may never make the book clubs. But he has tumbled a very large Humpty Dumpty from a very high wall of history, and American historical literature will never be entirely the same, despite king's horses and king's men."

WANTED--DEAD OR ALIVE

· For

a hatchet job on

Charles
Beard

Reward--$100,000

(contact A.H.A.
c/o Merle Curti)

Card prepared and posted by one of Forrest's graduate students

The *New York Times* did not review the book. Instead it editorially quoted my effusive dedication to Fulmer and Fulmer's jacket-blurb praise of me and added the comment, "just friends." But shortly afterward, C. Vann Woodward, in reviewing another book for the *Times*, began by saying "Because no one has done the kind of meticulous analysis of the Jacksonian period that Forrest McDonald has done for the Constitution, it is still possible to write books like this." Subsequently, in the Phi Beta Kappa *Key Reporter* (April 1959), Woodward wrote of *We the People* that "no historian will thenceforth embark on a venture of economic interpretation without prayerful contemplation of this work."

I was told that at the meeting of the American Historical Association in December 1958 the president (or perhaps he was the president-elect) of the organization, Merle Curti, was going around telling anyone who would listen not to pay attention to *We the People,* for

December 7, 1960: Forrest on NBC's "Continental Classroom." Photo by
Kas Heppner

"after all, McDonald is a tool of the power trust, you know." The
comment fell on deaf ears; the verdict expressed by Potter and
Woodward was all but unanimous. Another president, Robert
Livingston Schuyler, wrote of me in a February 1961 review article
in the *Journal of Southern History* that "a new star has appeared
in the firmament of American historiography." Eventually even the
New York Times came around. In the *Times* on November 28, 1965,
Dan Boorstin reviewed the paperback edition favorably, noting "the
gargantuan scholarly labors."

That was heady stuff for a kid who had written the book when
he was twenty-eight years old. During the early 1960s I had occasion to be thankful that my original goal as a jock had not worked
out. The star pitcher for the University of Texas Longhorn baseball
team when I was there was Bobby Layne, who went on to everlast-

ing glory as the quarterback for the Detroit Lions. Bobby and I were freshmen together and were the same age; indeed, it was he who had demonstrated to me that I could not hit a curve ball. By the early 1960s Bobby's career was coming to an end, and the Lions traded him to the Pittsburgh Steelers. In a story about the trade, *Time* magazine referred to him as "the ancient Bobby Layne." At the same age, I was a raw rookie in the history game.

■

FIVE

A Barefoot Boy in the Ivy League, and a Lot of New Players

When I received my appointment at Brown, I was not only a mere stripling compared with the old pros in the game, I was actually younger than historians my own age, in a manner of speaking. Most of my contemporaries in graduate school and as a tyro professional had spent three to five years in the armed services during the war, whereas I had served just a year and a half. They were somewhat older and more mature than their predecessors had been, and they worked the newly available troves of primary sources with gusto and skill.

As a consequence, they turned out monographs that undermined the New Historians' interpretive edifice, brick by brick. By the time I left Brown in 1967—after a checkered but essentially happy and heady eight and a half years—a fresh synthesis was possible and in order. But the profession was changing, and for a variety of reasons, that was not to be.

I shall be considering this bevy of new players and their works at length, but let me get to my part of the story first. When I went to Brown University in 1959, it was not the richly endowed, faddish, radical chic institution it would become by the late 1970s. As the sixth oldest college in the country, on the eve of commemorating its bicentennial, Brown was steeped in history and was conservative in its educational philosophy. Except for a fluffy innovation called I.C., for Identification and Criticism of Ideas, which had been established by President Henry Merritt Wriston, Keeney's predecessor, the curriculum was traditional, and students were required to take a considerable range of courses. Brown aimed at and produced a broad, old-fashioned liberal arts education.

Its graduate program fell short of the undergraduate program. Brownies attended other graduate or professional schools, and there they flourished. Graduate students at Brown had received their undergraduate degrees elsewhere, and on the whole they were neither as well educated nor as intelligent as the Brown undergraduates.

The faculty was a mixed bag. Perhaps a fifth of the members published at least occasionally, and a few, such as Jim Hedges and Leon Cooper, a Nobel Prize winner in the physics department, had earned renown. Younger colleagues, such as William G. McLoughlin, a historian of religion in America, were starting what would prove to be distinguished careers. Most of the faculty, even if they were not scholars, were dedicated teachers, and the members of the classics department were superb pedagogues. And yet, almost every department had dead weight, people who did not publish and were mediocre teachers. The worst was the chairman of the political science department, who had been at Brown since taking his Ph.D. at Harvard thirty years earlier. He never published a line, and during his first year he had written out his lectures, which he read to his classes, unchanged, year after year after year.

The ambience was a bit stuffy and stodgy. Politically, the faculty was vaguely and lukewarmly liberal. With exceptions, the older members were also vaguely anti-Semitic. Rumor was that Brown had a quota system for Jewish undergraduates, though I never encountered evidence of it. But I can illustrate the atmosphere by

Brown University, 1962: Forrest holding office hours

reference to a couple of minor episodes. Once the history department was considering applicants for the graduate program, and by far the best candidate was a graduate of Brooklyn College named Jerome Sternstein, whose photograph indicated that he looked even more Jewish than his name sounded. Several older members were disposed to dismiss his application out of hand, but when I put up a strong argument in his behalf, they backtracked lest the real reason for their opposition surface. On another occasion, I asked Hedges to recommend a physician to cope with a back problem I was having. He suggested someone but added, "Now I should warn you that he's Jewish, but he really is very good."

The truly wonderful thing about Brown in those days was its undergraduate students. Roughly a quarter of the 3,600 undergraduates were females, who had their own college, Pembroke, situated on the opposite side of the campus from the men's dormitories and fraternity houses. Pembrokers expected to be employed for a while after college, but few aspired to careers. Instead, they were trained to be well-educated, poised, and proper young ladies who would be hostesses and ornaments to the professional men they would marry. To become such, they endured a variety of curfews, parietal rules, dress codes, and set-aside "gracious living" days. And the process worked: forever afterward, Pembrokers remained charming and graceful people.

The males were another story. "Cool" was much in vogue among them, which meant that they must never appear to take anything too seriously, except sports. Their aspiration, as far as studies were concerned, was to earn no higher than a "gentleman's C." That was not easy, for their intelligence levels were extremely high, higher on average than the members of the faculty. The occasional nerd actually studied, or more properly allowed himself to be detected in the act of studying. The ideal can be illustrated by a student named Gerry Boyle, a handsome, Boston-Irish hockey player. Each course at Brown normally required a term paper; Boyle set for himself the formidable task of graduating without writing a single original paper, and through the exercise of ingenuity and charm he succeeded in the undertaking.

As for teaching, my course load was one undergraduate lecture class and one graduate seminar per semester, which left me abundant time to continue doing research and writing. I completed the Insull biography about a year and a half after arriving in Providence, and it was published by the University of Chicago Press late in 1962. Insull's life was replete with drama, starting with his humble origins in London, going on to his finagling his way into a position as Thomas Edison's private secretary, attaining a vice presidency of General Electric at the age of thirty-two, pioneering the development of the electric utility industry, winning fame and fortune by creating a utility empire extending over more than thirty states, then collapsing spectacularly in 1932, and being denounced personally by

Franklin Roosevelt. He was indicted, tried for fraud, and acquitted. "For his fifty-three years of labor to make electric power universally cheap and abundant, Insull had his reward from a grateful people: he was allowed to die outside prison."[1]

The story provided me the chance to write something that could appeal to nonspecialists, and I must say I did a smashing job; the book reads like a novel. Indeed, though the overwhelming majority of reviews were favorable, one reviewer, a plodding business historian, wrote that the book read so well it couldn't be good history because everybody knows that business history is dull. The book did not accomplish what I had hoped for, however. The standard textbooks in American history had depicted Insull as the archetype of the high-flying dishonest businessman of the 1920s. After my book came out, instead of revising their texts to give Insull credit for his achievements, the authors simply removed him totally from their books.

One mishap occurred in connection with publication. For once, Roger Shugg made a miscalculation, underestimating the potential sales. He decided on an initial press run of 7,500 copies, that being an enormous quantity for a university press; a typical university press monograph sold fewer than 500 copies. But *Insull* sold out in weeks and was on the *New York Times* best-seller list. The advantage of being on the list is that the reading public buys the book precisely because it is a big seller. Unfortunately, Shugg could not get a second printing done until after Christmas, and by then my opportunity to make a killing had passed.

Before moving on, I would like to quote a passage from the preface to *Insull*, for, though it may seem pretentious, it expresses something central to my creed as a historian. But first, I must indulge in a further digression. I teach my students never to use long quotations, for publishers insist that any quotation longer than three or four lines must be set solid, which is to say indented on both margins and hav-

---

1. Forrest McDonald, *Insull* (Chicago, 1962), 333.

ing no spacing between lines. When one encounters them in a book, one simply skips them. But now, I am going to violate my rule in the expectation that I have enough clout with the publisher to have the copy set in the ordinary way, as if I were not quoting, and in the hope that the reader will actually read the quote, not skip it.

In the preface I mentioned a number of Very Important Persons whom I had interviewed as part of the research and pointed out that "each said, Sit down, I'll buy you a drink (or I'll take you to lunch, or another equivalent, each according to his way)." After a long time, "I realized that in buying me a drink each sought in his own way to buy my memory.

"For an even longer time I puzzled: Why should anyone, and particularly these giants of the earth, want to buy my memory? And then one day I knew: The reason is that they viewed me not as a person at all but as an institution. They saw my coming as the Day of Judgment, and thus to them my memory was the memory of History; it was the memory of mankind; perhaps it was even the memory of God. This is what everyone, in his own way, sought to buy. Titans and paupers, tycoons and proletarians, those who have won and those who have lost; all wanted to distort or destroy—to fix—that part of the past in which they had lived. This is why they wanted to buy my memory.

"But my memory is not for sale. Not for drink, nor money, nor even for love. I am both fallible and corrupt, but my memory, though fallible, is incorruptible."

A brief additional digression is in order, one that may appear to be unrelated to a book about the historian's craft and my part in it. Not long after we arrived at Brown my wife became mentally ill and was committed to an institution. In intensive psychotherapy after her release, she became convinced by her psychiatrist that she wanted a divorce. I strongly resisted, but to avoid a messy court trial I eventually consented.

The development was instrumental to my career as a historian for strange reasons. In the property settlement I agreed to pay her alimony, child support, and a housing allowance that amounted to the total of my current net salary. Consequently, I had to live on whatever I could scare up by such odd jobs as editing manuscripts, plus advance royalties on books I contracted to write. If one is to live on royalty advances, one must deliver quality manuscripts regularly and frequently. Thus any inclination I might have had to stop producing and rest on my laurels was overruled.

The other relevant by-product was more complex. As it happened, I was teaching summer school at Columbia when the divorce proceedings were filed; I had a leave of absence from Brown for the academic year 1962–1963 and, having a Guggenheim Fellowship, I planned to spend the year in a remote, inexpensive place working on a sequel volume to *We the People*. Early on at Columbia I encountered a Pembroke junior named Ellen Shapiro whom I had had in class and who was truly the best student I have ever had. She was taking summer courses at Columbia, and she ended up going to Spain with me while I worked on the book. On the day my divorce became final, August 1, 1963, we were married and have been ever since.

She finished her degree and set about making herself invaluable to me. She taught herself how to type, she attended virtually every class I taught over the better part of four decades, she often team-taught with me, she took over the role of mother when the children came into my custody, she became the sole person I trusted to do research for me, she has managed the household and my correspondence, she has come up with the ideas for most of my books, and she edits what I write. As I wrote of her in a preface, there may be no such thing as an indispensable man, but there is an indispensable woman.

On to the new players and their works. Not every major contributor was a rookie in the sense of being young or recently admitted to the guild. Bray Hammond, a banker by profession, spent almost twenty

Christmas Day dinner, 1962: Forrest and Ellen at Pepe Rico's house in Nerja, Spain; their first picture together

years on the Federal Reserve Board before publishing, at the age of seventy-one, a book entitled *Banks and Politics in America from the Revolution to the Civil War,* which won a Pulitzer Prize in 1958. Tom Govan was fifty-two when *Nicholas Biddle: Nationalist and Public Banker* was published in 1959. Together, their works made mincemeat of *The Age of Jackson* by Arthur Schlesinger, Jr. As was indicated earlier, Schlesinger had reinterpreted the Jacksonian period as the manifestation of eastern, urban, working-class, and intellectual reformers and a precursor of the New Deal, instead of as the frontier phenomenon depicted by the Turnerians.

Between them, Hammond and Govan demonstrated that Jackson's policies were destructive, not only to the national government but also to the frontiersman and workers whom historians had described as the movers and prime beneficiaries of Jacksonian democracy. In regard to particulars, Hammond and Govan were largely in agreement, but in certain areas they disagreed. To put it simply, Hammond depicted the Jacksonians as knaves and fools because they were a band of unscrupulous state bankers and businessmen, based mainly in New York, who were moved by the get-rich-quick spirit of the times and sought to profit by casting off the central government's restraints. Govan's work, finely focused and intensively researched, weakened Hammond's larger interpretation somewhat by demonstrating that few of Jackson's principal supporters were opposed to the Bank. Rather than representing a knavish conspiracy of businessmen, they were just fools. Govan reported that the Jacksonians' destructiveness arose from a well-intentioned but slavish dedication to the dogmas of Jeffersonian republicanism and a desire to purify America by restoring an imaginary pristine past.

Either way, Hammond's and Govan's work pointed out, without being explicit, the fundamental flaw that plagued the writings of the New Historians: their utterly unsophisticated conception of economic activity as the exploitation by the wealthy of the poor, laborers, farmers, and small businessmen. That, as Hammond and Govan showed, was not how money was made. Rather, entrepreneurship, ingenuity, luck, and hard work created wealth, and the entire society benefited, albeit unequally. Those who ran to government seeking to bring business under control were driven by self-interest or by ignorance, it does not matter which.

In the same vein was the work of relatively recent specialists, historians of American business enterprise. Earlier writers had, of course, dealt with the subject from a muckraking point of view. Shortly after the war, however, there emerged a group of scholars interested in understanding rather than castigating. For the most part, they were connected with the Harvard Business School, which revised its curriculum to adopt a case-study approach. The resulting concentration upon how specific businesses actually operated entailed a sympathetic historical approach. Historians at the B School spread their influence by instituting a scholarship program whereby young historians could go to Cambridge and be trained in business history and by promoting its first-rate journal, the *Business History Review.*

Members of the B School faculty turned out influential works in their own right. Ralph Hidy, for example, wrote a history of the Weyerhaeuser company, showing that that organization, far from being the ruthless destroyer of America's natural forests, was committed to a program of conservation and reforestation that would have done Theodore Roosevelt proud. Fritz Redlich authored an excellent monograph, *The Molding of Modern Banking,* which paved the way for Vincent Corosso's history of the investment banking business. Henrietta Larson and Arthur H. Cole likewise made contributions that helped transform robber barons into the captains of industry they had been.

Innovation came from a host of sources, some of them unlikely. Consider, for example, the works of the students of Paul Wallace Gates at Cornell. Gates was a historian of the American West, a specialty that was still regarded as de rigueur at major universities. He was a left-winger who was convinced that the story of the West was a tale of continuous exploitation by eastern capitalists, railroads, and speculators, but as a teacher of graduate students he had a superb record because he attracted good people and let them report what they found, even if that went against his cherished prejudices. Thus, for instance, in 1955 Allan Bogue published *Money at Interest: The Farm Mortgage on the Middle Border* and reported that western farmers, far from being bled by eastern moneylenders, as Gates had held, enjoyed comparatively low interest rates and their creditors went to extremes to avoid foreclosures. Leslie E. Decker, in *Railroads, Lands, and Politics: The Taxation of the Railroad Land Grants* (1964), showed, contrary to Gates' depiction, that western farmers loaded railroads with taxes. Morton Rothstein (in "America in the International Rivalry for the British Wheat Market, 1860–1914," *Mississippi Valley Historical Review,* December 1960) demonstrated that western farmers, rather than being the hapless victims of an exploitative marketing system, as Gates had taught, were beneficiaries of a system so cheap and efficient that they could compete in international markets with overseas producers who operated on the basis of significantly lower production costs.

Various studies were sponsored and subsidized. During the 1940s the directors of the Social Science Research Council, curious as to whether the notion that nineteenth-century America was a laissez-faire society was true—clearly, from the 1830s to the late 1890s the federal government made little effort to regulate the economy besides stimulating it by tariff policies and land grants—authorized studies of particular states. The results included Oscar and Mary F. Handlin's *Commonwealth: A Study of the Role of Government in the American Economy: Massachusetts, 1774–1861* (1947); Louis Hartz, *Economic Policy and Democratic Thought: Pennsylvania, 1776–1860* (1948); James S. Primm, *Economic Policy in the Development of a Western State: Missouri, 1820–1860* (1954); and Milton S. Heath, *Constructive Liberalism: The Role of the State in Economic Development in Georgia to 1860* (1954). In each instance, the stereotypical notion was overturned, for state regulation and intervention in economic activity were the norm.

One could grow positively giddy describing all the breakthrough work published by the postwar generation of American historians who exploited sources recently made accessible. Instead, let us turn to a group of historians whose work was cumulative rather than exploitative and resulted from deep and imaginative thinking rather than intensive digging.

A case in point is that of Richard P. McCormick. Settling into a lifetime career at Rutgers University even before he completed his pioneering book on New Jersey, he produced further studies of the state's history. One of these, published in 1953, was a history of voting in New Jersey. That led, in turn, to a rethinking of the origins of the American party system and to a realization that Beard's book on the subject was irrelevant, for the Jeffersonian-Federalist division did not long endure. The successor schism, associated with the Jacksonians and their enemies, was a different phenomenon that, with permutations, survived and continued to prevail into modern times. McCormick expounded this interpretation in *The Second American Party System: Party Formation in the Jacksonian Era* (1966). The study has not been surpassed, though it can by enriched by reference to Chilton Williamson's *American Suffrage from Property to Democracy* (1960) and Edward Pessen's *Jacksonian America: Society, Personality, and Politics* (1969).[2]

Perry Miller's output followed a similar pattern. His early books, *Orthodoxy in Massachusetts* (1933) and *The New England Mind: The Seventeenth Century* (1939), excited the few readers who could abide his turgid and verbose style, though Miller's colleague, Samuel Eliot Morison, thoroughly panned them. Fourteen years later he followed with *From Colony to Province,* almost at the same time as McCormick's study of voting in New Jersey. Much richer and more readable was his *Errand into the Wilderness* (1956), a collection of essays covering religious attitudes and practices throughout the American colonies.[3]

Another powerful thinker who shaped the change in outlook, though he published little, was Douglass Adair. Adair took his Ph.D. at Yale in 1943 with a dissertation, "The Intellectual Origins of Jeffersonian Democracy." Unpublished during his lifetime, this dissertation was nonetheless widely read and frequently cited. After a brief

2. Another important and enlightening book that enriches our understanding of parties during the Jacksonian period is Lawrence Frederick Kohl, *The Politics of Individualism: Parties and the American Character in the Jacksonian Era* (New York, 1989).

3. For Perry Miller, see the chapter by Robert Middlekauff in *Pastmasters: Some Essays on American Historians,* ed. Marcus Cunliffe and Robin W. Winks (New York, 1969), 167–190.

stint of teaching at Princeton in 1946, Adair became a teacher at William and Mary and took on the editorship of the *William and Mary Quarterly*. Until 1955, when he left Virginia to become a professor at the Claremont Graduate School, he refashioned the *Quarterly* and turned it into the foremost journal in the field of American history prior to 1800.

Along the way, in addition to being instrumental in launching a number of scholars on careers of considerable influence, he published major articles. These included "The Authorship of the Disputed Federalist Papers" (1944), "The Tenth Federalist Revisited" (1951), " 'That Politics May Be Reduced to a Science': David Hume, James Madison, and the Tenth *Federalist*" (1956–1957), "The Jefferson Scandals" (1960), " 'Experience Must Be Our Only Guide': History, Democratic Theory, and the United States Constitution" (1966), and "Fame and the Founding Fathers" (1967). In his articles, Adair foreshadowed and stimulated the development of the ideological school of the founding of the American Republic, closely associated with Bernard Bailyn, Gordon Wood, and J. G. A. Pocock, but including Trevor Colbourn, Caroline Robbins, and Gerald Stourzh. Most notably, Adair demonstrated the influence of seventeenth-century English radicals and eighteenth-century Scots upon the thinking and works of the Framers.[4]

Then consider C. Vann Woodward, who did not so much revise an existing interpretation as create an interpretation where none had existed before. Southern historians had written copiously about the antebellum period, the Civil War, and Reconstruction, but as for what happened after "Redemption," they were eerily silent. In a vague sort of way, those who thought about the South in the half century after the end of Reconstruction opined that the section was primarily agrarian, presided over by a benign group of "Bourbons"—largely

4. *Fame and the Founding Fathers: Essays by Douglass Adair,* ed. Trevor Colbourn, with a memoir by Caroline Robbins and a historiographical essay by Robert E. Shalhope (New York, 1974).

former planters committed to the ideals of Thomas Jefferson—whereas the North was industrial, in the grip of rapacious robber barons. Woodward, instinctively opposed to simpleminded constructions, did his best work in refuting this version of Reconstruction.[5]

His first book, growing out of his doctoral dissertation, was a biography: *Tom Watson, Agrarian Rebel,* published in 1938. Watson was a populist leader in Georgia who perceived that the Bourbons were a group of robber barons themselves, and he strove mightily to form a coalition of small farmers, black and white, in an effort to wrest power from them. He failed, and in the long run he became a rabid racist, but that did not affect Woodward's point.

Woodward served as an intelligence officer in the navy during the war.[6] Afterward, he returned to the study of the South, and in 1951 he published two influential books. In *Reunion and Reaction: The Compromise of 1877 and the End of Reconstruction* he accounted for the disputed 1876 Hayes-Tilden presidential election by tracking elusive evidence that southern politicians had connived with northern republicans to have the last federal troops removed from the South and incidentally to be rewarded with assorted plums from the federal government. *Origins of the New South, 1877–1913* was volume nine in the Louisiana State University Press series *A History of the South.* Both works became classics and remain standard interpretations.

Those books established Woodward's credentials, and he settled down to writing articles and comments about the historian's craft and responsibilities.[7] But he had a last interpretive arrow in his quiver, *The Strange Career of Jim Crow* (1955). As an undergraduate at Emory in the late 1920s and early 1930s, Woodward (along

5. For Woodward, see David M. Potter, "C. Vann Woodward," in *Pastmasters,* 375–407.

6. In that capacity, Woodward wrote a remarkably lucid book, *The Battle for Leyte Gulf* (1947), describing the reconquest of the Philippines in 1944.

7. C. Vann Woodward, *The Future of the Past* (New York, 1989), collects some of these pieces.

with David Potter, Tom Govan, and a number of other intelligent and sensitive young men) had become incensed by Jim Crow and passionate in reaction to it. The racist southern historian Thomas Perkins Abernethy expressed a widely held view when he cackled that they were "unsound on the nigra question." They could do little but protest, and protesting was career-threatening as long as they remained in the South. Glenn Rainey, a friend who was teaching English at Georgia Tech, was vociferous on the subject, and the state legislature reduced the yearly appropriation for the school by the precise amount of Rainey's salary, specifying his name in the legislation.[8]

Then came 1954 and the decision in *Brown* v. *Board of Education,* and the long battle for desegregation loomed. Segregationists insisted that segregation was natural, that it had existed voluntarily on the part of both races from time immemorial, and that social mores could not be legislated. During the fall after the *Brown* decision, Woodward delivered a series of lectures at the University of Virginia in which he developed a theme that he had briefly stated in *Origins of the New South,* namely, that the legal structure of segregation had not existed in fully developed form until states began enacting comprehensive legislation a full generation after the end of Reconstruction. The essays were published a year later as *The Strange Career of Jim Crow.*

The book itself had a strange career. It went through a number of editions, each selling more than the last. The thesis that most of the Jim Crow statutes had been enacted in the 1890s and after the turn of the century went largely unchallenged, though Charles Wynes (1961), Frenise Logan (1964), and Joel Williamson (1965) demonstrated that such legislation had been enacted in Virginia, North Carolina, and South Carolina in the 1860s. Moreover, Richard C. Wade showed, in *Slavery in the Cities* (1964), that segregation had existed long before the Civil War in southern towns. In the face of this evidence, Woodward was forced to amend, hedge, and qualify

8. Potter, "C. Vann Woodward," 376.

his generalizations. The book, in the end, turned out to be an example of a historian's letting what his heart told him influence what his research showed him. To Woodward's credit, he retreated from his original position and incorporated subsequent research into his revised editions.[9]

The work of Richard Hofstadter was in a class of its own. In an exchange with him in the *American Historical Review* (1965), I offered the respectful suggestion "that Professor Hofstadter—who has given us a host of brilliant *interpretive* works—may be somewhat out of contact with the new breed of younger historians," who "have been doing the grubby, tedious work of digging up data." The judgment may seem harsh, but after reviewing his major publications, I feel no need to change it.[10]

As an undergraduate at the University of Buffalo in the 1930s, Hofstadter majored in philosophy and history, and though for his graduate study he shifted totally to history, his work continued to be more nearly philosophical than conventionally historical. He took his Ph.D. at Columbia and remained at that institution throughout his career. Life in the radical atmosphere of New York City during the Great Depression marked him deeply. He acquired an enduring fascination with politics and the influence of economic interests upon politics. His first book, *Social Darwinism in American Thought* (1944), stressed ideas rather than economics, but his second, *The American Political Tradition and the Men Who Made It* (1948), declared that "modern critical scholarship" had "reached a high point in Charles A. Beard's *An Economic Interpretation of the Constitution,*" labeling it in his bibliographical essay "a great study." In a 1954 essay, he praised Beard's historical method and chastised the profession for not adopting it. Yet his 1956 review of Robert E. Brown's book on Beard for *Commentary,* while objecting to the

9. Ibid., 398–399.
10. Arthur M. Schlesinger, Jr., "Richard Hofstadter," in *Pastmasters,* 294.

"often unnecessarily polemical and censorious" tone, concluded that "the historiography of the future will be much closer" to Brown's work than to Beard's.[11]

Perhaps Hofstadter's most influential book was *The Age of Reform: From Bryan to F.D.R.*, first published in 1955. He had earlier advanced the idea that American reform movements usually contained a nostalgic element, a longing for a return to a lost golden age, and here he added an explanatory thesis, that of the "status revolution." The Populists, he suggested, were disgruntled farmers concerned not so much with their economic interests as with their steady decline in status following urbanization and industrialization. Their program was essentially negative, not positive; they were anticity, anti-capitalist, anti-Semitic, anti-immigrant, anti-progress. The same was true, Hofstadter opined, of the leaders of the Progressive Movement, who were middle-class people living in towns and small cities whose former status as community leaders was being undermined by the rise of the merchant princes, the great industrial capitalists, and their lackeys. Their program involved using the federal government's power—which otherwise they distrusted—to break the power of the trusts. Only with the advent of the New Deal did a reform movement turn to the federal government for positive action, and even the New Deal was partly motivated by status insecurity, though economic insecurity was at the heart of it. Hofstadter offered a formula: in times of economic troubles, interest politics tended to prevail, whereas in prosperous times (such as the 1950s, when McCarthyism flourished), status was more potent.[12]

For a while, the status interpretation gained widespread acceptance, but then it began to come under an onslaught from scholars who were doing, or had done, "the grubby, tedious work of digging

11. Ibid., 281; Richard Hofstadter, *The American Political Tradition and the Men Who Made It* (New York, 1948), 15, 349; Richard Hofstadter, "Charles Beard and the Constitution," in *Charles A. Beard*, ed. Howard K. Beale (Lexington, Ky., 1954), 75–92.

12. Richard Hofstadter, *The Age of Reform: From Bryan to F.D.R.* (New York, 1961), 131–172.

up data," rather than offering explanations of what was supposed to have happened. Norman Pollock defended the Populists from the charge of anti-Semitism. Richard Sherman demonstrated that in Massachusetts the Progressives and their enemies were recruited from the same social classes. Joseph Huthmacher showed that in New York immigrants and Progressive reformers were often allied. More decisively, C. Vann Woodward, who had been through the Populist Movement with Tom Watson, blasted his friend Hofstadter's interpretation.[13]

As this exciting work was being done, I was not entirely idle myself, though I managed to become sidetracked. I finished the first sequel to *We the People,* and it was published as *E Pluribus Unum.* The book traces the story of American politics at both the national and state levels from the Declaration of Independence through the adoption of the Bill of Rights. The story, looked at closely, is rather seamy, for what most political figures were doing much of the time was pursuing power and profit, and their methods were sometimes sordid. The outcome of their pursuits, however, was grand, and those "giants" of 1787 "spoke in the name of the nation," not in the name of regions or states or countries or towns, "and the people followed them. As a result, the Americans were, despite themselves, doomed forever to be free."[14]

Though it elicited a bit of caviling, the book was favorably received, but two curiosities marked the reception. For the *New York Times* Esmond Wright penned a genuine rave—a "fresh, vivid and penetrating re-creation of the crucial 14 years in which a new nation was born," for example—and the piece was unusually long. At almost any other time, such a review would likely have been the lead

13. W. T. K. Nugent and M. P. Rogin reached similar conclusions. Schlesinger, Jr., "Richard Hofstadter," 460–461; C. Vann Woodward, "The Populist Heritage and the Intellectual," *American Scholar* 24 (1959), 55–72.

14. Forrest McDonald, *E Pluribus Unum: The Formation of the American Republic, 1776–1790* (Indianapolis, 1979 [first ed., Boston, 1965]), 371.

in the *Times* book review section, thus stimulating book sales, but the *Times* workers were on strike that summer, and when publication resumed after Labor Day, the editors jumbled the accumulated reviews into a single massive edition. Consequently, Wright's encomium was buried. (I was not destined to get rich off my early writings, though a later Liberty Press edition of *E Pluribus Unum* continues to sell.)

The other peculiarity was that many reviewers commented that, having demolished Beard's economic interpretation, I had put my own economic interpretation in its place, had "outbearded Beard." Indeed, in his essay "Fame and the Founding Fathers," Douglass Adair referred to me as Beard's "young follower." He wrote that he would give my book "two cheers—but only two cheers." The first cheer was for showing "with a complete persuasiveness that at issue during the Critical Period, running like a dirty thread through the warp of state politics and the woof of national politics, was the desire" of many prominent figures "to enrich themselves by both legitimate and illegitimate manipulation of political power." The second cheer was for my showing, "as no historian before, how economic appetites and greed in *state* politics between 1783 and 1787 threatened to destroy the fragile Union of the Articles" of Confederation, and for giving "a far more sweeping and a far more sophisticated picture of the dynamic interrelationships of avarice and American politics than Beard's simple-minded" division into capitalists and agrarians.[15]

Adair withheld his third cheer, he wrote, because I had defined self-interest too narrowly. Specifically, he declared that the selfish drive for Fame—the secular substitute for Christian immortality in the form of grateful remembrance by posterity for one's nation-making efforts—drove many of the Founders. Adair was absolutely right.

E Pluribus Unum was published by Houghton Mifflin. I had signed on with a superb literary agent, Sterling Lord, and Sterling

15. Colbourn, *Fame and the Founding Fathers,* 4, 22, 23.

put together a multibook contract, including a schedule of wholesome advances. The next book was to have been a biography of the investment banker Jacob Schiff, a contemporary of J. P. Morgan and leader of the Jewish investment banking community from the 1880s until his death in 1920. Schiff was an extremely interesting man and was, until the outbreak of World War I, more powerful and influential than Morgan himself. I did the necessary research in the Jacob Schiff Papers at Hebrew Union College in Cincinnati, but I never wrote the book. Years later, I bought my way out of the contract by returning the unearned portion of the royalty advance.

The main reason I did not write about Schiff was that, as I said, I got sidetracked: I signed a contract to write a textbook on the history of the United States in the twentieth century. *The Torch Is Passed* was published in 1968 by Addison-Wesley, a company based in Reading, Massachusetts. The book laid an egg, and I am not sure why. It is tolerably well written and is a handsome volume. Part of the reason was perhaps that it was Addison-Wesley's maiden venture into history; the firm had been quite successful in the fields of science and technology but did not know the history market. For whatever reason, *Torch* earned back the substantial advance they had paid me, but little more.

By that time I had conceived a larger project. With Leslie Decker I would write, and Addison-Wesley would publish, a survey of the full course of American history in two or three volumes, incorporating into a synthesis the best monographic literature of the preceding two decades. Decker knew the nineteenth century, I knew the period up to 1800 and after 1896, so the collaboration seemed to make sense. But we were a shade too late, for the study of history was about to move in radical directions.

And so was I. My departure from Brown came about as follows. Brown had adopted a small black college in Mississippi called Tougaloo; it sent some professors down there to lecture and from time to time brought a handful of students to Providence for a semester. I was outraged by the blatant racism of the project, and on October 28, 1964, in a debate with a colleague about the pending presidential election (I was a supporter of Barry Goldwater against Lyndon Johnson, whom I correctly predicted would be a disaster), I voiced my opinion about the Tougaloo program. I considered the venture to be profoundly immoral, on the grounds that it patronized the blacks and provided a fraudulent cover-up for Brown's lack of black students. (The administration maintained that qualified blacks could not be found; I offered to fill the entire freshman class with qualified blacks, an offer that was scornfully dismissed.) My principal reason, however, was that if the project had any effects, they would be to raise the hopes and expectations of the Tougaloo students far beyond what was remotely possible in the context of Mississippi society—and that was a cruel and dangerous undertaking. If Brown really wanted to do something for the blacks of Mississippi, I added, it would try to educate Mississippi whites. It happened that James Farmer, the head of the Congress of Racial Equality, came to town a few weeks later and said pretty much what I had said, and also substantial criticism along the same lines came from Tougaloo.

But to my colleagues I had spoken heresy. A special meeting of the faculty (to which I was not invited) was called within hours. Rejecting a sentiment shared by the more zealous champions of civil rights that a lynch party be organized, but determined to demonstrate to the world that Brown was a Tolerant Liberal Intellectual Community, the faculty voted unanimously to disassociate itself from my statements and to endorse the university's position. As closely as I could ascertain, this was the first time the Brown faculty had been unanimous on a question of public moment since the hysterical days of World War I, when it had resolved that teaching German was un-American and patriotically voted to revoke the honorary degree it had earlier awarded to a German statesman.

A couple of weeks later, President Barnaby Keeney sent me a letter seconding the vote of the faculty, telling me that it "might, indeed, have been much more strongly worded" and informing me that my behavior "leaves open the question of the appropriateness of your membership on this faculty." He subsequently made clear to me that I would never receive another salary increase at Brown.[16]

I stayed around for a while waiting for an acceptable opportunity. Then in 1966 Wayne State University in Detroit offered me a professorship at half again my Brown salary. I accepted, and we moved in the fall of 1967.

In the interim, life in Providence was pleasant enough, for our relations with the students were close and happy, but an unfortunate development took place, namely, turnovers in the history department. Carl Bridenbaugh was hired, and shortly thereafter Jim Hedges died. Many people thought that landing Bridenbaugh was a coup, for he was a well-known colonial historian and president or former president of the American Historical Association. Furthermore, he was coming to Brown from Berkeley, at a time when California was raiding the Ivy League on a large scale. I had serious misgivings about the quality of his work, and he soon demonstrated that he was a sorry excuse for a human being.

His first action on arriving at Brown was to persuade the department to refuse tenure to its medievalist Tom Bisson, a young scholar destined to become a superstar who had taken a sabbatical leave after having been promised that he would be awarded tenure upon his return. In his place the university proposed to hire a big-name medievalist and crony of Bridenbaugh's from Berkeley. Bill McLoughlin and I fought Bridenbaugh tooth and nail on the matter, but in vain, and he conceived a bitter hatred toward us. And this is the kind of person he was: he took out his hostility on our students.

16. Letter dated November 13, 1964, from Barnaby C. Keeney to Forrest McDonald, in McDonald's possession.

I had a graduate student, John Head, who had done a fine dissertation that had already been accepted for publication, but Bridenbaugh attempted to prevent Head from getting his degree. McLoughlin had a student named Jack Bumstead, and for years Bridenbaugh wrote nasty letters to prospective employers in an effort to prevent Bumstead from obtaining a decent job.

Accordingly, I left with mixed feelings. I sorely missed the Brown students and Rhode Island, but I was happy to be getting out of that foul academic environment. Little did I suspect that that kind of environment would come to prevail throughout academe.

SIX

■

The Sixties, Seventies, and a Bit Beyond

When we arrived in Detroit in August of 1967, the city was on fire and had been for two weeks. The civil rights movement had reached a zenith in the mid-1960s with the enactment of the Civil Rights Act of 1964, Martin Luther King's march from Selma to Montgomery, and the Voting Rights Act of 1965, but already ultra-radical black leaders had appeared. First came the black-is-beautiful campaign, then the black-power movement, and then an explosion in the form of random violence, looting, and burning of inner cities across the land. In 1964, Harlem, Brooklyn, Rochester, Jersey City, Paterson, and Elizabethtown exploded. The next summer, rioting rocked the Watts section of Los Angeles, and in 1966, mayhem erupted in at least eight cities. Detroit was the climax.

Along the way, white radicals who had supported civil rights groups were driven from the movement, and simultaneously the Vietnam War escalated. On college campuses throughout the country, students—though exempted from military draft—joined with their young assistant professors to protest the war. Soon they, too, became radical and violent. Sit-ins, teach-ins, and trashing of campuses proliferated, inspired by a conviction that the United States was a perfectly vile country and always had been. Concurrently, females discovered that not just Indians, blacks, and other minorities had been oppressed by a cruel, rapacious, capitalistic society, but women as well.

The disruptions on campuses came to a sudden halt after May 1970, when several students were killed at Kent State University in Ohio and Jackson State in Mississippi, but the spirit of radicalism and alienation perdured. The result, as far as the study of history was concerned, was an awakened interest in subjects that historians had previously slighted. Indian history, black history, women's history, family history, and a host of specializations arose.

These expanded horizons enriched our understanding of the American past, but they also resulted in works of special pleading, trivialization, and downright falsification. And the older generalizations, together with the excellent monographs that had recently been published, were thrust aside as irrelevant. To compound the problem, the waves of vandalism, combined with thefts by collectors and genealogists, provoked manuscript repositories into imposing restrictions on the use of their collections.

Clio, the muse of history, was clearly facing turbulent times.

The Wayne State University campus was not on fire when we arrived. Indeed, the university had no campus; it consisted of a grouping of buildings surrounded by business establishments. The huge student body—almost 50,000—was collectively apolitical, consisting mainly of young men and women who paid their own tuition by working on assembly lines and hoped through education to better their lot. The sole demonstration took place when the administration foolishly tried to close for a few days in the wake of Kent State. The students were paying to attend classes, and they wanted what they were paying for.

My initial encounter with Wayne students was curious. My undergraduate survey course covered a third of United States history, from the mid-eighteenth century to the end of the Jacksonian period. On the opening day I decided to describe the general conditions in the colonies circa 1750, and I asked whether the students were familiar with the topography, climate, and vegetation along the eastern seaboard. None of them was. I therefore delivered an hour-long description, which they seemed to follow with interest.

Afterward, a junior came up to me and introduced himself by saying, "Dr. McDonald, there are a few points from your lecture that I'd like to ask you about." Thinking here was an opportunity to learn something about the student body, I suggested that we go to the commons, where he could ask his questions over a cup of coffee. When we had settled in, he asked his first question: "You talked about tidewater country. What does that mean?" I explained that it was the coastal plain, called "tidewater" because the rivers rise and fall with the flow and ebb of the tides. He looked bewildered, and I added, "You know about the tides, don't you?" He asked in return, "Is it like the current in a river?"

Having just come from Narragansett Bay, I was well versed in how the tides worked, and I proceeded to explain the matter to him. I told about the gravitational pulls of the sun and moon and how they worked in tandem sometimes and at cross-purposes at others, and how at certain seasons such as the vernal and autumnal equinoxes they were stronger than at other times. He listened, utterly rapt, and when I finished, he said, "Gosh. That's really interesting, Dr. McDonald. But I don't understand this history stuff. I'm a science major, myself."

At that moment I said to myself, "Okay. You're not at Brown anymore." But that was not all. As time passed I came to realize that what was going on in higher education was a general dumbing down to accommodate the enrollment of people who had no business being in college. Wayne State had equal status under state law with the University of Michigan and Michigan State, but it was in reality a bloated community college. Wayne had a good faculty and a strong history department, but in keeping with the trend toward getting everybody into college, as if that were a universal right, Wayne was part of a movement that saw the proliferation of community colleges and junior colleges and the pretentious rechristening of colleges as universities. Necessarily, standards had to be lowered as enrollments increased. Symptomatic of the malaise was that Wayne instituted scores upon scores of remedial classes to make up for what students had not learned in grammar school and high school.

Accompanying the lowering of standards was, more or less inevitably, grade inflation. A grade of C was, by definition, average. What was average at Wayne was far lower than what was average at Brown, but even allowing for that, the pressure to raise grades was enormous. After we diluted the contents and watered the requirements, the problem should have taken care of itself, yet it did not. I can offer an example that illustrates the whole. In my spring survey course, I was approached by a middle-aged undergraduate who told me that she had to have a C in my course if she were to get her degree. I checked the grade book and found that she was marginally passing. When she took the final, however, she clearly failed it. I was faced with a dilemma. She was a welfare recipient, and the state was paying her way. If I failed her, she would keep on enrolling at public expense until somebody gave her the needed C, and she would graduate anyway. I debated with myself as to what was the proper thing to do, then decided to give her the F she had earned. The decision was not an easy one.

I did not know it at the time, but grade inflation was not confined to schools like Wayne State; it was the beginning of a nationwide phenomenon that would go on for decades until, in some instances, the average grade had become a B plus.

Now as to where the study of history was heading. The first historical revisionism to emanate from the black-is-beautiful campaign was not the work of professional historians and was, to say the least, rather outré. It consisted mainly in pronouncements that various historical figures whom everyone had always assumed to have been white were in fact black. The ancient Egyptians, for example, were solemnly declared to have been black. So, too, was Alexander the Great, and I dimly recall hearing that Aristotle was a black philosopher. Nor were revelations confined to the ancient world: a declaration announced that Ludwig von Beethoven was black. Another strand purported to prove that American industrial capitalism had been built by slave labor. Though palpably absurd, such revisions could be justified as socially useful myth-making, something akin to Kwanza.

Of the serious scholars in the field of black history, few were of African descent. Among those who were, by far the most prolific and able was John Hope Franklin. Franklin took his B.A. at Fisk and earned his Ph.D. at Harvard. He taught at various black institutions for a time, went on to become chairman of the history department at Brooklyn College, then spent a number of years at the University of Chicago before moving to Duke. His field was American history, not exclusively black history, and among his major works were a textbook, *From Slavery to Freedom: A History of Negro America,* which went through numerous editions; *Militant South* (1956); *Reconstruction after the Civil War* (1961); *A Southern Odyssey* (1976); and *Racial Equality in America* (1976). Franklin was, despite his unique angle of perception, perfectly in the mainstream of American historiography. His work on Reconstruction, for instance, though written from a different point of view and influenced by the radical W. E. B. DuBois, was roughly similar in its broad outlines to Dunning's 1907 version.

Of the white historians of American blacks, some turned out works that were as inane as the fantasies conjured by the black-is-beautiful school. Kenneth Stampp, for instance, rewrote the history of Reconstruction with a radical twist. His account of the course of events was the same in almost every detail as the older versions, but he turned the interpretation upside down. Earlier versions depicted Reconstruction as a tragedy because Radical Republicans had tried to go too far, too fast, and had left the white South devastated as a result. Now, Radicals were attacked because they did not go far enough, fast enough, and long enough to ensure racial justice for the freedmen. What they should have done was make the Freedmen's Bureaus into powerful permanent agencies, redistributing the land and acting as guardians and protectors of the freedmen. According to Stampp, the tragedy of Reconstruction was that the blacks and the Radicals did not triumph. Stampp's myth-revising book is "a bald illustration of Becker's dictum that each generation rewrites history to suit its present prejudices."[1]

By contrast, a great deal of the black history written by whites in the 1960s and 1970s was of high quality. Earlier, when blacks were mentioned, either slave plantations were presented as being like concentration camps, or, more commonly, blacks were treated as simpleminded sambos. Now, sympathetic studies began to depict them as real human beings leading real lives. Among the many who made contributions from a variety of perspectives were Winthrop Jordan, Sam B. Hilliard, and Philip Curtin.

The best of them, in my opinion, at least in regard to the history of blacks under slavery, is Eugene Genovese. At that time Genovese was a staunch Marxist, but unlike some Marxists I have known, he has a flexible mind and a keen imagination and is utterly immune to self-deception. His work, most notably *Roll, Jordan, Roll: The World the Slaves Made* (1972, 1974), was based upon an awesome

---

1. Kenneth M. Stampp, *The Era of Reconstruction: 1865–1877* (New York, 1965). Woodward belittled the speculations of armchair revolutionaries about what might have been had the federal government been more active; he pointed out that everything desired for the freedmen had been put in place in regard to the western Indians, and yet they fared worse than the blacks (C. Vann Woodward, *The Future of the Past* [New York, 1989], 196–198). See also Forrest McDonald, "Conservative Scholarship and the Problem of Myth," *Continuity* 4/5 (1982): 65.

range of research, and it demolished a number of clichés, including those of the Mammy, the emasculated male, matriarchy, and the obsequious "house nigger." Building upon a thorough knowledge of the Bible and of Christianity, together with an uncanny understanding of the psychology of paternalism among masters as well as slaves, he showed how blacks made themselves into a society of normal human beings under utterly abnormal circumstances.

More controversial was the work of Robert W. Fogel and Stanley L. Engerman, *Time on the Cross: The Economics of American Negro Slavery* (1974). Fogel and Engerman were representatives of an innovative method of historical study called quantification, econometrics, or cliometrics—analysis of subjects through the use of numbers. They concluded that the slaves were well fed and clothed, comfortably housed, and adequately medicated. The slaves, though oppressed, were less exploited than free industrial workers in the North and in Europe, received a larger real income, and had a longer life expectancy. Maltreatment was rare, whippings were few, broken families unusual; the integrity of the family was fostered, and slave breeding was almost nonexistent. Slave labor was more efficient and productive than that of free farmers in the North and brought about one of the richest and fastest growing economies in the world. These conclusions shocked most readers, but though numerous and fierce attacks were launched against the book, the profession in general was simply cowed by the numbers.

So enamored did historians become with the riches to be mined through cliometrics that a generation experimented with the technique. Little of consequence was learned as a result, and happily, the profession largely abandoned the approach. Unfortunately, our sister discipline, political science, has been almost wholly converted to it.

Members of the still-dominant liberal establishment were baffled by the recent findings of the historians of American blacks: things were simply not as they had seemed. The liberals were as nonplussed by the works that emanated from another group of historians who came to be known as the New Left.

In the realm of foreign policy, the liberals were aware that American political leaders had flirted with imperialism during the late nineteenth and early twentieth centuries, hence the occupation of the Hawaiian Islands, the Spanish-American War, the annexation of the Philippines, McKinley's talk about teaching our "little brown brothers" the blessings of democracy, and Teddy Roosevelt's corollary to the Monroe Doctrine. But such impulses, in the view of most, were aberrant; under Wilson and again under FDR, the United States resumed its benign and exemplary role in international affairs. By the New Left's reckoning, the real story was quite otherwise.

As indicated earlier, the leading historian of this school was William Appleman Williams. Williams' far-reaching works included *The Tragedy of American Diplomacy* (1959, revised editions in 1962, 1972, and 1981) and *The Contours of American History* (1961). The gist of his interpretation is that the United States was imperialistic almost from the beginning, despite its protests to the contrary and its efforts to end the imperialism of rival nations and that its own imperialism exacted a heavy toll on the inhabitants of its "colonial possessions" and led the country into repeated wars.

The process of reasoning whereby Williams arrived at that interpretation was roughly as follows. In the seventeenth century, even as the English colonies in America were being settled, the concept of universal rights of private property was being developed in the mother country. The notion was potentially disruptive of the ideal of the brotherhood of Christian believers, and its advocates cautioned against the danger. John Calvin opined that a man might choose among callings but was bound by God's law to follow the one that promised the greatest public good. John Locke taught that a man could accumulate property, but only insofar as he could consume it and none went to waste; the rest belonged to the public. Locke's patron, Lord Shaftesbury, a dedicated advocate of mercantilism, insisted that merchants who made themselves rich but did not contribute to the welfare of England as a whole were vicious sinners. Settlers took these attitudes to America with them.

But a condition in America ensured that the limitation on property rights would be ineffective: the frontier. The presence of open, free land provided, in Turner's phrase, a "gate of escape" from responsibility toward the community. For four decades after independence, American leaders remained committed to mercantilism, in the sense of using governmental power to harness private greed to serve the public good, but then the system broke down and was replaced by a *Weltanschauung* that Williams called *laissez nous faire*. Under that world outlook, as the nation extended itself across the continent, phenomenal economic growth took place, the proceeds being shared unequally. Some individuals grew excessively wealthy, largely by obtaining special favors from Jacksonian-style politicians; urban laborers were exploited unmercifully, though they never became militantly radical because they had the safety valve of the frontier.

Toward the end of the nineteenth century, three developments brought profound changes: the frontier closed, the form of economic activity moved from individual entrepreneurship to corporate dominance, and the nation's capacity to produce far outstripped its capacity to consume. Given these circumstances, Williams believed, Americans should have abandoned their accustomed ways and set out to make their society more equitable and just. Instead, they sought a substitute for the frontier in overseas expansion. They announced the Open Door Policy for China and extended it to the entire underdeveloped world. Americans professed that their motives were altruistic, that they were encouraging improvement and self-determination. In the end, however, the subject lands found themselves economically worse off, and self-determination meant remaking oneself in the image of America.

Moreover, Americans thought they could achieve their goal of expanding markets without becoming involved in imperialistic wars. However, economic expansion led directly to war. The United States entered World War I because it feared that the Germans were going to take away markets in Latin America. A generation later, the severe economic recession of 1937, which undid the modest gains the reformist New Deal had made, convinced FDR and the country that a resumption of expansion was the way to end the Great Depression. Williams did not entirely subscribe to Charles A. Beard's theory that Roosevelt conspired to get the United States into the war—nor, for that matter, to Harry Elmer Barnes' and Charles Tansill's conspiracy theories of American entry into World War I—but his interpretation differed in detail, not in general substance.[2]

Like Williams' work, much of the domestic history produced by the New Left was cast in the form of angry accusations, amounting to an indictment of the entirety of the American past. Like his work, too, theirs contained some kernels of truth and a measure of plausibility. Two works published in 1976 spring to mind as illustrative of the genre: Gabriel Kolko's *Main Currents in American History* and Page Smith's *A New Age Now Begins: A People's History of the American Revolution.*[3]

---

2. As for the origins of the Cold War, Williams declares that it is pointless to argue about who started it, but as he tells the story, the blame is clearly to be placed upon the United States. His *American-Russian Relations, 1781–1947* (1952) shaped the New Left's view on the subject and was expounded by a number of other New Left historians. *Diplomatic History: The Journal of the Society for Historians of American Foreign Relations* (Spring 2001) has an informative roundtable discussion about Williams' work, including James Livingston, "Social Theory and Historical Method in Williams' Work"; Justus D. Doenecke, "Williams and the Anti-Interventionist Tradition"; and Patricia Nelson Limerick, "Williams and Western American History."

3. The ensuing paragraphs follow fairly closely the observations I made in reviewing the two books, Kolko's in the *National Review,* September 17, 1976, 1015–1016, and Smith's in the *Virginia Quarterly Review* 54 (Autumn 1976): 701–706. Lest the reader suppose that such works were not taken seriously, consider this: in 2003, a similar book, Howard Zinn's *A People's History of the United States,* sold its millionth copy. Christopher Flannery, "No Limbaughs on the Left," *Claremont Review of Books* (Summer 2003): 9.

A number of Kolko's generalizations echo sentiments long held by conservatives. Governmental interference in the economy is bad, unions do not do much to help workers, Social Security is regressive and dysfunctional, and Lyndon Johnson's War on Poverty was hokum. He points out what I and various others in treating business history had shown, that the movements between 1880 and 1920 to regulate public utilities and businesses such as meatpacking arose from the affected businesses themselves.

But this is part of Kolko's larger indictment of American capitalism. He maintains that capitalism in the United States outlived its destined time because immigrant industrial workers, trying to earn enough money to return to their home countries, never developed an appropriate class consciousness, and because big business, acting under the guise of liberalism, joined in unholy alliance with big government and big military. Having thereby become incredibly powerful, capitalistic America staggered about the earth as an ailing colossus, blindly destroying the innocent peoples of the world in a futile effort to keep its hideous corpus alive. These judgments are couched in Marxist cant and the patois of the social sciences and are flavored by the mandatory use of statistics.

When unwelcome reality resists obfuscation, Kolko turns it into an accusation. The structure of capitalism places limits upon what workers can be paid! In America, unions failed to obtain wages that transcended those limits! American capitalists undermined class consciousness by paying workers the highest real wages in the world!

And finally, Kolko echoes Williams' claim that corporate capitalism has given the United States a virtual world monopoly on violence and personal and social disintegration—a proposition that can be sustained by the simple expedient of ignoring the history of every other society that has existed.

Page Smith was a mainstream historian until, at some point in the 1970s, he embraced radical chic. To folks of that persuasion, women's lib, gay lib, Indian rights, back to nature, ecology, communal living, consumerism, and four-letter words were "in"; government, corporations, the military, the bureaucracy, conventional morality, stability, and social order were instruments of repression and exploitation. These and similar bromides mark the interpretive gist of Smith's *People's History of the American Revolution*. America had been settled by the oppressed classes of Europe, by transported convicts, and by "hippies and dropouts." In the seventeenth century they read the radical pamphlets of Levelers and Diggers, whose ideas fell "like seeds in a welcoming soil" and "became as familiar as the Bible." Trouble started in the 1760s, when the decadent British ruling class set out to suppress American liberties; the American masses responded by rising in the world's first "people's liberation movement." (Never mind that the Maccabees came a bit earlier.) Their rebellion was justified: "The excluded or repressed are always right in their rebellion, for they stand for our future wholeness." The Boston Tea Party was "guerrilla theater." When the war came, American officers blundered, but the enlisted men (and the many women who participated) were brave, unflinching, and "willing to bear far greater physical hardship than the professional British soldier"; they fought for their liberties, whereas the Brits fought merely for their "wretchedly low pay." The position of the Americans is described as being comparable to that of twentieth-century Vietnamese fighting against the United States.

Quite in addition to the hundreds of gross factual errors, the book teems with bizarre judgments. "Every great enterprise begins in love, not in political arrangements or legal definitions." The pro-American Whigs in Parliament "saved Britain from a social revolution more ferocious and destructive than the French Revolution." And most telling for me, Smith says that there is something about a chained dog that brings out the sadist in us all.

The book appealed to fashionable prejudices and was taken seriously enough to be chosen a Book-of-the-Month Club selection. Worse yet, it was not atypical of the historical writing of the time.

And the liberal establishment, in regard to such writing, rolled over and played dead.

The radical swing of the historical profession pretty well insured that the textbook I was writing with Leslie Decker would be a commercial dud, if indeed it had not been a chimerical project from the onset. Teachers were no longer interested in the solid monographs that had been published since World War II; the subject matter that held their interest had changed completely. Moreover, a large percentage of the instructors who taught the survey courses were junior members of a radical persuasion, and though they were not always the people who chose the texts—sometimes the department made the choice—they constituted a sufficient proportion of the market to prevent our book from selling.

The venture was ill-fated for another reason as well: Decker did not carry his share of the load. As I said earlier, the plan had been that Decker would write the nineteenth-century chapters, and I would do the eighteenth and twentieth centuries. The seventeenth-century chapters were to be a joint effort. As it worked out, Decker wrote one and a half of the thirty-five chapters, and I wrote the rest. To compensate for the unequal load, Decker agreed to do the index, a sizable undertaking for a book of more than a thousand pages. That proved to be catastrophic. He turned the task over to his wife, who complied it on a computer that picked out everything beginning with a capital letter except for the first words of sentences. In addition to yielding some ridiculous personal and place name entries (for example, I had written of Jefferson's foreign policy that he could control every coast "from the Florida keys to Hong Kong" but that would be meaningless without the British navy's permission to use the seas—and Hong Kong found its way into the index[4]), the

4. Forrest McDonald, Leslie E. Decker, and Thomas P. Govan, *Last Best Hope: A History of the United States* (Reading, Mass., 1973), 309, I–16. The Florida Keys escaped inclusion in the index because in the text "keys" was lower case.

method ensured that the index would have no subject entries. When teachers inspect a textbook, they automatically check to see if subjects that interest them are discussed. Mrs. Decker's index would have told them that there was nothing on their subjects.

In one regard, Decker did carry his weight. He had moved from the University of Maine to the University of Oregon, where he became a colleague of Tom Govan. We persuaded Tom to cosign the text in exchange for working with Decker in making an exhaustive survey of the literature published on the subjects covered in each chapter, making sure that everything in the book reflected the best recent research. That assured accuracy and made possible an innovation. After every four chapters we put in a "Summary and Historiographical Note," which included a running account of what had been published over the years.

Though the book did not sell well, I was pleased with the product. Addison-Wesley published it in 1972 as *The Last Best Hope: A History of the United States,* the title being derived from Lincoln's second annual address to Congress. It appeared in a two-volume issue for colleges on the semester system, in three volumes for those on the quarter system, and in a single volume for what market I know not. As a result, I am vague when people ask me how many books I have written. Do I count *Hope* as one, two, or three? In any event, even today I am still comfortable with the book. It is handsome, for Addison-Wesley's design people were superb, and it is readable, which can rarely be said about texts. Its interpretations bear up under informed scrutiny, and in certain matters it is, I believe, the best that has been written—for instance, chapter twenty-seven, entitled "Humpty-Dumpty and the King's Men: The Coming of the Great Depression."

The experience of *The Last Best Hope* soured my relationship with Decker, and our friendship essentially came to an end. One would suppose that might have been sufficient to discourage me from entering into a collaborative project again, but another began shortly after the Decker fiasco. This one was with my friend and colleague Grady McWhiney, a distinguished southern historian, on what would come to be called the Celtic thesis.

The idea evolved slowly and erratically at first, but it gained momentum over time. In 1973 Grady had published *Southerners and Other Americans,* in which he pointed out various ways in which antebellum southerners and northerners resembled each other, but even before the book was in print, he was dissatisfied with his inability to account for the reasons that southerners differed from northerners. Ever curious, he set about attempting to learn why, but the undertaking was elusive on account of the nature of the documentary record: whereas northerners wrote prolifically about what they thought and what they were doing, southerners did not, which in itself turned out to be an important clue. What was abundantly available, however, were accounts of the southern people written by outsiders who traveled through the South. Making due allowance for the possibility that such accounts were biased, but reckoning that outsiders would be likely to record things that were strikingly different, he began an exhaustive study of these records.

Along the way, he came across an interesting datum that had been neglected in conventional works on the South: the region raised enormous quantities of livestock, especially hogs. Lewis C. Gray, in his monumental two-volume *History of Agriculture in the Southern United States to 1860* (1933), had covered livestock raising, and Frank L. Owsley, in his admirable *Plain Folk of the Old South* (1949), had devoted twenty-eight pages to the subject, but both Gray and Owsley treated animal raising as a transient thing, conducted either on the frontier or by people who aspired to be tillage agriculturalists and ultimately plantation masters. Grady was skeptical. Such a reading did not square with the observations of travelers, for animal raisers were as numerous in the older parts of the South as in the West, and they were described as being singularly lacking in aspiration toward upward mobility.

Grady found accounts of something that virtually no historians had described. Each year, in late summer, enormous herds of animals were rounded up and driven long distances to market. Moreover, a goodly number of tillage farmers raised Indian corn as their cash crop, the corn being sold to herdsmen along their routes to market. Indeed, the routes were sprinkled with "hog hotels," established solely to service the hog and cattle drives. I can remember Grady's holding forth amusingly at parties, especially after having a drink or two, on the glamour of the hog drives, declaring that John Wayne should make a movie as a hogboy rather than as a cowboy.

In the meantime, I was toying with a nebulous subject that had occurred to me sometime earlier. When we lived in Spain, Ellen and I had noticed the extreme differences that persisted among the inhabitants of the various regions of the country—Andalusians, Murcians, Catalans, Basques—even though Spain had been unified in 1492, four and half centuries before. It occurred to me that if different parts of Spanish America had been settled by people from different parts of Spain, that might account for the variations in the histories of Spanish-American countries. I remembered enough Spanish-American history to know that the countries varied considerably, but not enough to check out my hunch. I discussed the question with several Latin American historians but got nowhere.

Sooner or later I realized that the kinds of variations we had seen in Spain had probably existed in the British Isles as well and that the effects would have been evident in colonial America. I asked Carl Bridenbaugh if such variations had pertained in the British Isles, and he replied, "Of course." But when I pressed him for details, he dismissed me. Then one day I happened to be reading a textbook history of England written by my Wayne State colleague Goldwin Smith, and I came across a peculiar thing. About a third of the way through the book, Goldwin had produced a map of Britain showing the distribution of peoples around the time of the Norman Conquest. A couple hundred pages later, another map appeared, showing the distribution of Cavaliers and Roundheads—supporters of the Crown and of Parliament, respectively—during the English civil war of the 1640s. Astonished, I went down the hall and showed the two maps to Goldwin. He said, "By Jove! They are identical, aren't they?" They showed a line running northeast from Cornwall in the southwest of England, the southern and eastern half being lowlands, the west and north being uplands.

Forthwith, I began reading histories of Ireland, Scotland, Cornwall, and Wales as well as of England, concentrating on economic and social history. This taught me that the north and west, the historically Celtic countries and England's "Celtic fringe," had been populated mainly by animal raisers, and that the southeastern half had been characterized by tillage agriculturalists.

Grady and I put our heads and our findings together, and two conclusions occurred to us at once. First, we were dealing with the same people, which is to say that his antebellum southern herdsmen were the descendants of my herdsmen in the uplands of the British archipelago, who, when emigrating to America, had taken their accustomed ways with them. The second was that the herdsmen in both places were not tillage farmers who supplemented their farming with herding, nor were they people who hoped by hard work and frugality to become something different from what they were.

We were acutely aware that these observations ran counter to what for many years had been the prevailing interpretation of the American experience advanced by Frederick Jackson Turner in his 1893 essay "The Significance of the Frontier in American History."[5] Turner used the word frontier, which in Europe meant the boundary

5. Forrest McDonald and Grady McWhiney, "In Search of Southern Roots," *Reviews in American History* (December 1977): 456–457.

between countries, to denote an irregular line between the settled and unsettled portions of British North America that became the United States. Beyond it lay a vast but ever-shrinking area of free land, and the existence of that free land transformed Americans into an individualistic, independent, and democratic people. It prevented strains when hard times hit the settled areas, for if workers in the East faced economic hardship, they could readily pack up and head for the "safety valve" provided by the open land in the West. Such cultural baggage as frontiersmen took with them, whether from the East or directly from Europe, was rapidly worn away by the necessity of adapting to a new environment; the pioneering experience created a new breed of men.

Appealing and enduring as Turner's thesis was, it runs counter to common sense. A moment's reflection is enough to indicate what, above all else, the vacant spaces of the American frontier provided that was lacking in Europe: places where people could by choice live among persons like themselves and apart from persons who differed from them. In such enclaves they could retain their accustomed ways, whereas those who remained in settled areas were subjected, from the seventeenth century though the nineteenth, to a combination of changing events, circumstances, and pressures that made resistance to cultural change almost impossible. In sum, the New World did not create a new man; it enabled men to remain what they had been.

As Grady and I learned upon reading the works of cultural anthropologists, we had here a classic instance of cultural conservatism—the tendency of a people to continue to think and behave in customary, socially conditioned, and familiar ways unless war, conquest, technology, interaction with alien groups, or other forces necessitate change, and the tendency to retain or revert to those norms in modified form despite the forces of change. We also had an example of cultural preadaptation or preselection—the concept that over the course of time a society will develop combinations of traits and habits that have survival value in a particular human or physical environment, and if the members are placed in a different environment, they will fare well or ill in proportion to the compatibility between their traditional ways and their new surroundings. The Celtic and Celtic-fringe people had evolved ways that, by the seventeenth and eighteenth centuries, had become less suitable to survival in the Old World, but when they moved to a wide-open America, their ways permitted them to thrive.

To tie the parts of the thesis together, we had to analyze colonial immigration patterns. Though studies of the subject were not as numerous or as thorough as they were soon to become, and though we had not yet devised a method for analyzing the ethnic distribution of the population at the first census in 1790, enough information was available to check the matter on a tentative basis. The major immigration to New England took place between 1625 and 1642, and it overwhelmingly originated in the southeastern part of Britain; that was, after all (as Goldwin Smith's map had indicated), Puritan and Parliamentary country. As for Celtic migration, the great wave of Scotch-Irish immigrants began after 1715 and continued at least until the American Revolution, and James G. Leyburn had shown (in *The Scotch-Irish: A Social History* [1962], a pioneering work that we subsequently learned was flawed in important particulars) that most of the Scotch-Irish debarked in Philadelphia, migrated toward the nearby uplands, then streamed southwestwardly down the valleys to Maryland, Virginia, the Carolinas, and Georgia. That gave us enough to go on.

We published our first article in the *Journal of Southern History;* it was entitled "The Antebellum Southern Herdsman: A Reinterpretation." We pointed out that livestock raising was a massive enterprise, the value of southern livestock in 1860 having been more than twice as great as the value of the cotton crop. After considering how our fellow historians had treated or mistreated the subject, we indicated that the open range prevailed throughout the South, which is to say that anyone, even those owning no land, had the right to graze animals on the lands of others, and that plantation owners were forbidden by law to fence in anything except growing crops. We described the pig drives and found an excellent account in an unexpected place. Edmund Cody Burnett, the distinguished editor and historian of the Continental Congress, had grown up in the Scotch-Irish area of the French Broad River in eastern Tennessee, and toward the end of his life he published an account of hog driving in his home area based on his own memory and on interviews with old-timers who could remember the antebellum years. Along the way, we mentioned that the southerners' open-range method of raising livestock and driving it to market was a continuation of ways learned in the British and Irish uplands.[6]

Over the course of the next few years, we published a dozen or so articles and two books elaborating, expanding, and correcting the basic thesis. Grady wrote the books; we coauthored most of the articles, an exception being one that Ellen and I wrote together. This was a study, published in the *William and Mary Quarterly* (April 1980), of the ethnic distribution of the population in 1790. We employed a refined version of a name-analysis technique devised by the American Council of Learned Societies back in the 1920s, and our findings pretty well confirmed our original thought: New England was overwhelmingly populated by people from the English lowlands, the Middle States were a thoroughly mixed lot, and the South was predominantly of Celtic or Celtic-fringe origins. (We subsequently analyzed, but never published, each of the censuses up to 1860, the result being that the Celtic and Celtic-fringe proportion amounted to almost 70 percent in the interior South.)

6. Forrest McDonald and Grady McWhiney, "The Antebellum Southern Herdsman: A Reinterpretation," *Journal of Southern History* 41 (May 1975): 147–166; Edmund C. Burnett, "Hog Raising and Hog Driving in the Region of the French Broad River," *Agricultural History* 20 (April 1946): 95. At a regional meeting of the Philadelphia Society in New Orleans, Grady and I presented a paper and afterward were privileged to hear Andrew Lytle, who was in the audience, sing hog-driving songs that he remembered from his childhood.

Reaction to the publications was mixed. Among southerners in general and southern historians, except those specializing in plantation history, the response was enthusiastic. *Newsweek* and *Southern Living* did feature stories on our work, and we were invited to write an article for the popular British journal *History Today*.[7] A few people were harshly critical, most notably a historian at Washington University in St. Louis named Roland Berthoff. Berthoff had a wife who was Scottish, and he somewhat snobbishly resented our lumping Scots together with the lowly Irish under the rubric Celtic. He blasted away at us in various places, some of which we rebutted and some of which we ignored.

Berthoff did inspire us to clarify and elaborate our use of the term Celtic. To paraphrase a footnote to an article Grady and I published in the *American Historical Review*,[8] we did not in using the term mean to suggest a common genetic pool, for the peoples under discussion were clearly of different genetic mixtures. The Welsh obviously have different genetic stock than the Irish, for example, and Highland Scots had different bloodlines than Lowlanders. Rather, we spoke of peoples who shared a common cultural heritage—customary lifestyles, attitudes, and ways of doing things. Even in that sense, of course, the people we treated as Celtic were far from identical. But after considerable thought we concluded that it is proper to consider them as a single general group, different from the English, much in the way that Western culture is seen as distinct

7. Jerry Adler with Holly Morris, "Celts vs. Anglo-Saxons," *Newsweek*, August 10, 1981; *Southern Living*, May 1985, 166; Forrest McDonald and Grady McWhiney, "The Celtic South," *History Today* 30 (July 1980): 11–15. On September 5, 1980, Harper Lee wrote us a letter that began "This is a fan letter" in which she lauded the "excellence" of the *History Today* article; we cherish this letter.

8. Forrest McDonald and Grady McWhiney, "The South from Self-Sufficiency to Peonage: An Interpretation," *American Historical Review* 85 (December 1980): 1108. We use Celtic in a nongenetic sense, in the way that historians speak about black or African-American history. No one holds that the blacks in American have a single genetic background. Obviously they come from many tribes intermixed with white, Hispanic, and Indian bloodlines in varying degrees. And yet no one disputes that black history is a legitimate subject.

from Islamic culture, while recognizing that Swedes and Italians differ from one another, as do Moroccans and Saudis. We could have increased the accuracy of the designation by using Celtic to cover "people in the British Isles who were historically and culturally other than lowland English," but somehow that phrase is not catchy.

Another point, concerning just who the Scotch-Irish were, was published in an article I wrote alone, but it reported something that Grady and I had learned together. Traditionally, the Scotch-Irish were reckoned as descendants of the Lowland Scots that James I had settled on plantations in Ulster starting in 1610. Two things belie the tradition. First, none of the plantations was in counties Antrim or Down, from which practically all the emigrants to America came. Second, the inhabitants of those two counties were part of a subculture of warriors, seamen, and herders that had existed as a politically autonomous Lordship of the Isles until the end of the fifteenth century. They were a hybrid of Ulstermen, Hebrideans, and western Highlanders; they bore little relation to either the "mere" or pure Irish or the Scottish Lowlanders; and they were regarded as the most Celtic of the Celtic peoples.[9]

Grady's initial book on the Celtic thesis was coauthored with Perry D. Jamieson, a former graduate student of his. The title indicates its message: *Attack and Die: Civil War Military Tactics and the Southern Heritage* (1982). Southerners fought, they concluded, "with the same reckless abandon, using the same assault tactics, that had characterized their Celtic ancestors for centuries." Prudence would have dictated otherwise, given the advent of the breech-loading repeater rifle, for that turned the traditional ways into a form of suicide, but prudence was never the long suit of either Celts or southerners.[10]

His next book laid out the whole story. We had thought for a time

9. Forrest McDonald, "Cultural Continuity and the Shaping of the American South," in *Geographic Perspectives in History,* ed. Eugene D. Genovese and Leonard Hochberg (Oxford, 1989): 223–224, n. 13.

10. In *Attack and Die,* see especially pp. 170–191.

of coauthoring a single huge tome tracing the history of the Celtic peoples from ancient times to the South in the twentieth century, but we abandoned that plan, partly because it would have been ungainly and perhaps unreadable, and partly because the good stuff on the antebellum South was material that Grady had dug up. Accordingly, I wrote a twenty-one-page prologue to *Cracker Culture: Celtic Ways in the Old South,* sketching the history of the Celts from ancient times to the eighteenth century, and Grady alone wrote the book proper.

I can summarize his findings in a passage from his concluding chapter. "Eyewitness accounts of life in the United States before the 1860s," he wrote, "reveal vast and important differences between Southerners and Northerners. Throughout the antebellum period a wide range of observers generally characterized Southerners as more hospitable, generous, frank, courteous, spontaneous, lazy, lawless, militaristic, wasteful, impractical, and reckless than Northerners." These observers described Northerners as "more reserved, shrewd, disciplined, gauche, enterprising, acquisitive, careful, frugal, ambitious, pacific, and practical." The antebellum South was "a leisure-oriented society that fostered idleness and gaiety, where people favored the spoken word over the written and enjoyed their sensual pleasures," consuming prodigious quantities of tobacco and liquor. The Yankees, by contrast, "were cleaner, neater, more puritanical, less mercurial, better educated, more orderly and progressive, worked harder, and kept the Sabbath better." Throughout the book, Grady emphasized that the same differences had distinguished lowland Englishmen from Celts and inhabitants of the Celtic fringe.[11]

Some years before the appearance of *Cracker Culture,* both the McDonalds and the McWhineys had moved along once more, the McDonalds for the last time. I was comfortably ensconced at

11. Grady McWhiney, *Cracker Culture: Celtic Ways in the Old South* (Tuscaloosa, Ala., 1988), 268.

Wayne, we were ardent fans of the Detroit Pistons and Tigers, I was happily managing a little league baseball team, and though Ellen especially disliked the cold, we might have remained there but for a sudden development. The faculty voted to unionize, and I was simply too old to retool as a member of the working class.

I began to cast about for someplace to go; what we required was a decent university in a place with a mild climate. At the meeting of the Southern Historical Association I mentioned my availability to Aubrey Land of the University of Georgia, and he was excited by the prospect of hiring me. Shortly afterward, however, he wrote me that he was ashamed to say it, but his colleagues opposed the appointment out of concern that my publication record would make them look bad by comparison. So I continued to look.

Meanwhile, I had a sabbatical leave coming, and we made a decision. I would take two years off instead of one, the second without pay—I was confident I could get a research grant to take up the slack—and buy a farm in the deep South. We bought twenty isolated acres in the Florida panhandle and moved in May of 1974. I left only twice during the next two years, once to New York to promote a book I had written called *The Phaeton Ride: The Crisis of American Success*,[12] and once, ironically, back to Detroit to receive an award as Wayne's most distinguished faculty member. Otherwise, I dabbled with the Celtic thesis, read things I had never had time to read before (such as Blackstone's four-volume *Commentaries on the Laws of England*), and worked the land. We installed a super-sophisticated irrigation system, designed for us by the folks at the agriculture school of the University of Florida.

Laboring in the earth led to a project that had long-term ramifications. The very phrase reminded me of Thomas Jefferson's oft-quoted passage about those who labor in the earth being God's cho-

12. Forrest McDonald, *The Phaeton Ride: The Crisis of American Success* (Garden City, N.Y., 1974).

sen people, and it occurred to me that Jefferson would not have known this personally, since he had never labored in the earth himself, having had slaves to do it for him. But thinking about Jefferson inspired me with an idea. Earlier in 1974 I had published *The Presidency of George Washington* in the University Press of Kansas' series on the presidency, and I was curious as to who was slated to do the Jefferson volume. I telephoned the director of the press, and he informed me that he had been unable to find an author. Jefferson scholars, Jeffersonians all, did not wish to touch the presidency because Jefferson was by no means a Jeffersonian president. We agreed, therefore, that I should write *The Presidency of Thomas Jefferson*.

Whether Jefferson was a Jeffersonian president depends upon one's understanding of what Jeffersonian means. He was a many-faceted man who was given to extreme and sometimes crackpot utterances, especially among friends and in private correspondence. I once wrote of him that he reminded me of Walt Whitman's lines in *Song of Myself:* "Do I contradict myself? Very well then I contradict myself. (I am large, I contain multitudes.)" I was easier on Jefferson than Henry Adams had been, for I depicted his first term in office as a triumph; not until the final year of the second term did catastrophe overwhelm him. My greatest difference with Adams, however, is that Adams regarded the Jeffersonians as eminently forward-looking, staking all on the "doubtful and even improbable principle" that mankind could "become more virtuous and enlightened, by mere process of growth," in which case "no one could deny that the United States would win a stake such as defied mathematics."[13]

On the contrary, by my reading, the Jeffersonians were backward-looking, determined to resist the emergence of the modern world. They regarded Hamiltonian Federalism as an attempt to transform and corrupt the agrarian paradise that was America, even as the

13. Henry Adams, *The United States in 1800* (Ithaca, N.Y., 1955), 114.

August 1981: Forrest and Grady McWhiney on the front porch of the Southern History Center, University of Alabama

English Oppositionists had seen Walpole and the new monied classes transform and corrupt Old England. The Jeffersonians and their ideological forebears were reactionaries, swimming against the tide of history, for the world aborning was the depersonalized world of money, machines, cities, and big government. They succeeded in the short run, but over the long haul their cause was hopeless.

My favorite part of the book was the conclusion, where, after tracing the changing interpretations of Jefferson throughout the years, I wrote that "the real Jefferson—the one who once lived in Virginia and once worked in the President's House—was lost in the shuffle. So, too, was the America he wanted his country to become. . . . He and his followers set out to deflect the course of History, and History ended up devouring them and turning even their memory to its own purposes. History has a way of doing that."[14]

The publication of *The Presidency of Thomas Jefferson* in 1976 was, as Humphrey Bogart said to Claude Rains at the end of the movie *Casablanca,* the beginning of a beautiful friendship: Kansas has published every book of mine but one in more than a quarter of a century. The Kansas people are marvelous to work with, and I think they have not been entirely unhappy with the relationship.

By the time the Jefferson book was published, I had found my job in the South. Grady McWhiney had become chairman of the history department at the University of Alabama, and he asked me to join him. I agreed, though I confess that I had misgivings. Alabama, for goodness sake! But we bought twenty-plus acres outside of Coker and set about to fight the kudzu and teach our classes and write books. Finally we were home.

14. Forrest McDonald, *The Presidency of Thomas Jefferson* (Lawrence, Kans., 1976), 169.

■

SEVEN

The Grand (?) Finale

Shortly after we moved to Alabama, Oscar Handlin published a book called *Truth in History,* in which he almost despaired of the prospects for history as a subject and as a profession. When he had attended the annual meeting of the American Historical Association as a third-year graduate student in 1938, Handlin wrote, he had been powerfully impressed by the unity of purpose he saw there. Historians seemed dedicated to the pursuit of truth and appeared confident that cumulatively they would reach it, or at least an ever-closer approximation of it. That began to change in the 1960s, and by the late 1970s, Handlin was convinced that the dedication had disappeared.[1]

Though he couched his analysis in general terms, he did point out some horrible examples of recent work and named names. David Hackett Fischer's *Historians' Fallacies,* for example, Handlin casti-gated as "utter stupidity," declaring that Fischer got wrong the titles of books he criticized and made no effort to "read the books . . . to

1. Oscar Handlin, *Truth in History* (Cambridge, Mass., 1979), 3–24.

examine the accuracy of the statements he made about them." Handlin charged that Christopher Lasch's *The New Radicalism in America, 1889–1963* was riddled with "careless blunders." As for William Appleman Williams' *Contours of American History*, the book was so full of preposterous errors that Handlin laughed up-roariously and "could not altogether exclude the possibility that he intended it as an elaborate hoax. . . . Certainly large sections were altogether farcical. But they seemed not to be intentionally so, oth-erwise they would not have been interspersed with equally large, dull, and unhumorous ones." Gabriel Kolko, Lloyd C. Gardner, Robert Fogel and Stanley Engerman, and Norman Pollack received similarly caustic criticism.[2]

Handlin attributed the decline to several interrelated factors. Per-haps the most inimical were by-products of a boom in the demand for college teachers and particularly history professors. After World War II, college enrollments swelled enormously and, anticipating the maturity of the baby boomer generation, colleges and universities began to grind out Ph.D.s in unprecedented numbers. "The decade of the 1960s produced 5,884 doctorates as compared with 7,695 for the whole period 1873–1960." A decline in the quality of training necessarily followed, according to Handlin, not least because of the expansion of Ph.D. programs to institutions that had never offered the degree before. Earlier, seven prestigious universities had pro-duced nearly half of all Ph.D. degrees, but in the 1960s they pro-duced little more than a quarter of them. When Handlin had gone to his first meeting of the American Historical Association, the as-sembly was attended by 956 members. He gave up on the meetings in the late 1950s; the single occasion on which he attended another was in 1970, by which time the membership numbered in the tens of thousands.[3]

2. Ibid., 19–20, 145–146, 154, 206–224, 341–343.
3. Ibid., 23–24, 75–77, 4.

Accompanying the overexpansion and dilution of quality was a feeling of irrelevance that dispirited the profession. As waves of radicalism swept campus after campus, the students' persistent demand was that college education must be made relevant, though few students knew what they meant by the term. Political scientists, economists, and sociologists seemed better equipped to provide relevance than historians, but historians attempted to keep pace. Their efforts ordinarily took the form sought by student radicals, namely, an expansion into fields beyond the conventional and an emphasis on pointing out that the United States had historically been a rotten country.[4]

That development was compounded by the tendency to write and teach American history along the lines of good guys and bad guys. The tendency was by no means new; historians had been prone to tell their story in terms of good versus bad from the start. At the beginning of the twentieth century, the division had been rich people and their corrupt political supporters against the farmers, westerners, and working people they exploited. By the end of the century, the bad guys were white males of whatever class or economic background, and the good guys were blacks, women, Latinos, Native Americans, and homosexuals.[5]

Yet even the pessimistic Handlin was not willing to admit that the turn for the worse was irremediable. He deplored the good guys–bad guys approach, and he indicated that he feared that historians who wrote in those terms were highly selective in their research, but he doubted that they were palpably dishonest. Had he known of the woes that would rock the profession a generation later—an almost total loss of a sense of history among the young and revelations of plagiarism and outright falsification of evidence among historians—his despair, I daresay, would have been complete.

4. Ibid., 81–84.
5. Ibid., 332–352.

Despite all that has happened, however, I myself am a long way from despair. More Americans than ever before are buying and reading history. And, what is of equal importance, the cumulative march toward a greater understanding does continue.

I did not read Handlin's book when it first appeared, and had I read it I would have thought that he greatly exaggerated the gravity of the situation. As for the appalling ignorance of history among college undergraduates, I was personally unaware for a special reason. By choice, I taught the freshman survey course in American history, and without my realizing it, the 300 or so students I had each year were an unrepresentative sample of the student body. The course was not required of anyone except history majors, though the political science department, the business school, and advisors to prelaw students strongly recommended it. That meant that the majority of my students took the course because they wanted to, which presupposes that they already knew a good deal of history. They did, and I was able to use the class to recruit the brightest of them for my upper-level courses, which they took along with graduate students. They fared well at that level too, and accordingly, I labored under the impression that Alabama students were almost as good as Brown students had been.

Only after a dozen years did the University of Alabama institute distribution requirements, whereupon students from the weaker departments, such as education, nursing, and criminal justice, began to infest my classes. Forthwith, I was appalled by their ignorance: they did not know in which century the Revolution took place, and they did not know from what country the United States won its independence. After struggling with them for a few years, I stopped teaching the survey course. Thenceforth my students were upperclass history majors, meaning that the weakest had been filtered out before I had to deal with them.

In regard to the decline in the quality of the work professional historians were turning out, I was likewise insulated. To be sure, I read the pap being published by the likes of Williams, Kolko, and Page Smith—but only because I agreed to review it for one journal or another—and though I found it as bizarre as Handlin did, I regarded it as the exception rather than as an emerging norm. I could harbor that illusion because I have never made it a practice to keep up with the literature in my fields, as many scholars do. Instead, when I need to know what has been written on a particular subject, I send Ellen to the library, and she combs the books and journals and comes home with the best available studies.

Besides, I was aware of first-class history being produced by a number of scholars of various age groups. When I came to Alabama, for instance, among my junior colleagues was Howard Jones, who was launching a brilliant and prolific career as a diplomatic historian, and Tony Freyer, who was doing likewise in constitutional history. Among my elders in the profession, Dan Boorstin, Ed Morgan, John Lukacs, and others continued to produce excellent works, and among those my age or a bit younger, Pauline Maier, Robert Wiebe, Clarence Ver Steeg, Lance Banning, Elizabeth Fox-Genovese, and a host more were doing the same.

As for my own work, in addition to the Celtic thesis, I wrote an assortment of minor pieces, including a number of articles and a little book surveying American constitutional history, but I was growing antsy to undertake a major project. Ellen suggested a biography of Alexander Hamilton. When the first volumes of the definitive twenty-six-volume edition of *The Papers of Alexander Hamilton* appeared in 1961, the editors of the *William and Mary Quarterly* invited me to review the series as the books were published, and I had been doing that. The bulk of the research for a biography was thus substantially done, but before I started to write I plunged into one more research undertaking: I decided to read everything that I knew that Hamilton had read, the better to understand him. (When I told this to my friend Lance Banning, who was then deep into a research project on James Madison, he assured me that no one could do that for Madison; he was too widely read.)

Despite my preparation, however, the project started inauspiciously. I have always told my students that before they start to write anything—an article, a review, a chapter, or a book—they must sit down and map the whole thing, start to finish. In writing the Hamilton biography, I neglected to follow my own advice and instead simply started writing one chapter after another, more or less in chronological order. I had completed five chapters when, reviewing them in preparation for continuing to work over the Christmas holidays, I came to a sickening realization that they did not work: you could not get to Hamilton from there. I also realized that if I preserved them in the hope of salvaging copy, they would be a barrier to doing the job properly. Accordingly, on Christmas, Ellen and I spent the day in front of our Franklin stove, solemnly burning each page, page by page by page, until all were destroyed. The next day, I made a careful outline, and on the day after that I started writing from scratch.

As I was writing the book, a phase of my life as a historian was ending. Earlier, when I had submitted a chapter of my dissertation to Fulmer Mood and had received it back mutilated by his corrections and editorial suggestions, I asked him what I would do after becoming one of the big kids without a supervising professor. He said that I should find someone who is able and willing to serve as a thorough critic and rely upon him. For years, the someone who served me was Tom Govan, who was extremely generous with his time and help. In connection with the Hamilton biography, he was uniquely qualified to be helpful, for he knew and truly understood Hamilton. But there was a problem: Tom had terminal cancer. Nonetheless, I sent him the copy, chapter by chapter, and he read and revised it with his usual perceptiveness. He died a month or two after reading and criticizing the final chapter.

A postscript to this story: A mutual friend, upon hearing my account of it, opined that what Tom had done was wonderfully unselfish. I agreed, but I also thought—and his widow confirmed—that the experience of having a Hamilton manuscript to work on prolonged his life. And I add the following: throughout the years when Tom was reading and criticizing my copy, he never once said anything positive about what I had written. But when he returned the last Hamilton chapter to me, his final comment was, "Forrest, I can't tell you how happy it makes me that someone has finally got Hamilton right." Those were his last words to me.

As I interpreted Hamilton, his audacious, self-appointed mission was to remake American society in his own image. He saw that his adopted country was made weak and despicable by its citizens' narrowness of vision and lack of drive. Those shortcomings were reinforced by a social order in which status was derived not from the marketplace, where deeds and goods and virtues could be impartially valued, but from birthright. The system discouraged industriousness by failing to reward it and bred a people who (with few exceptions) had, as Hamilton put it, "the passiveness of the sheep." To Hamilton, this was anathema because it was inherently unjust. By 1787 he decided that he could accomplish revolutionary change through the office of the secretary of the treasury. What distinguished the industrious minority from the majority, in his view, was that they measured worth and achievement in terms of money. In order to transform the established order, to make society fluid and open to merit, what needed to be done was to monetize the whole—to rig the rules of the game so that money would become the universal measure of value—for money is oblivious to class, status, color, and inherited social position; money is the ultimate neutral, impersonal arbiter. Hamilton saw that by infusing money into a static agrarian order, it would become the leaven, the fermenting yeast, that would stimulate growth, change, prosperity, and national strength.[6]

6. This paragraph is adapted from Forrest McDonald, *Alexander Hamilton: A Biography* (New York, 1979), 3–4.

Liberals denigrate the society that resulted as being composed of grubby, materialistic, self-seeking, acquisitive individualists, and they denounce Hamilton as a champion of plutocracy. But they totally misunderstand Hamilton's genius. His commitment to private enterprise and a market economy was moral, not merely economic. He believed that the greatest benefits of his system were spiritual—the enlargement of the scope of human freedom and the enrichment of the opportunities for human endeavor. Thus he was the champion of liberty, of freedom under law, as opposed to those—the Jeffersonians—who defended privilege and authoritarianism.

By the time *Hamilton* was published, the bicentennial of Independence had come and gone and that of the Constitution was approaching. Richard B. Morris had written a piece in which he deplored that the first had been a somewhat insipid celebration and urged that the latter evoke genuine cerebration. Ellen suggested that I become a major participant in that cerebration, and I set out to write a lengthy analysis of the intellectual origins of the Constitution. The literature on the subject was not satisfactory, and I had another bee in my bonnet as well. Douglass Adair's comment that he would award *E Pluribus Unum* two cheers but not three had stuck with me and gnawed at me, as had his observation that I had omitted the intellectual dimension and failed to take into account the passion for Fame among the Founders. Accordingly, the time had come to rectify those shortcomings in the hope of earning a posthumous third cheer.

The Framers of the Constitution brought to Philadelphia in 1787 a common understanding. The proper ends of government were to protect people in their life, liberty, and property. They agreed that the proper form of government was a republic, though they were far from agreement as to what constituted a republic. They shared a knowledge of history and a tradition of the rights of Englishmen and the common law. They had at their disposal a huge body of political theory and at least some familiarity with a body of thought, political

Fall semester 2000: Forrest conducting an undergraduate seminar on the Constitutional Convention at the University of Alabama; Ellen is to the right. Photo by Catie McDonald.

economy, that had recently emerged. To be sure, they distrusted "speculative" theory. As John Dickinson said in the Convention on August 13, "Experience must be our only guide. Reason may mislead us." Theory, however, formed a fundamental base for their understanding and colored their perceptions of the past as well as the present. But there was a catch to this shared vision. Its "ingredients were incompatible." In the restructuring portion of their work theory was not relevant and "experience itself was inadequate: they could rely ultimately only on common sense, their collective wisdom, and their willingness to compromise." The result was "a frame of government that necessitated a redefinition of most of the terms in which the theory and ideology of civic humanism had been discussed"—a new order of the ages.[7]

7. Forrest McDonald, *Novus Ordo Seclorum: The Intellectual Origins of the Constitution* (Lawrence, Kans., 1974), 8, 262.

May 6, 1987: Forrest delivers the Sixteenth Jefferson Lecture in the Humanities, National Building Museum (Pension Building), Washington, D.C.

Thus was born my maiden adventure into the world of intellectual history—*Novus Ordo Seclorum: The Intellectual Origins of the Constitution*—though I had once been disdainful of the field and though it could be argued that *Hamilton* had been at least in part an intellectual history. My disdain for the genre, I should explain, had stemmed from my conviction that intellectual history tended to be the history of intellectuals, with but little relationship to real people, as it indeed had been when I was a young man. Since that time, a number of people had blazed a trail for a meaningful kind of intellectual history, and though *Novus* departed from the trail in important particulars, I was pleased with the way it turned out and would, in future, write more intellectual history.

First, however, I was diverted by the bicentennial cerebrations. Given the extravagant praise that reviewers bestowed on *Novus*, I expected

May, 1987: At the White House reception given by President and Mrs. Reagan the afternoon after the Jefferson lecture. Photo courtesy Ronald Reagan Library

that in the upcoming commemorations I would receive a goodly number of invitations to deliver addresses on the subject of the Founding, but I was unprepared for the deluge that occurred. The College of William and Mary offered me the James Pinckney Harrison Visiting Professorship for the 1986–1987 academic year. The salary proffered was a bit less than I was making at Alabama, but a housing allowance was included. I thought that an academic year in Williamsburg would be a pleasant experience, and I was honored by the invitation. I readily accepted.

Next came a huge honor: the National Endowment for the Humanities awarded me the Thomas Jefferson Lectureship for 1987. The Jefferson Lecture is the highest award the federal government gives for achievement in the humanities, and I was the sixteenth to receive it since it was initiated in 1971. Some of my friends feared that I might turn it down, inasmuch as I had been outspokenly critical of the Endowment and had gone on record saying it should be abolished. I had no intention of declining the honor, but I did not feel that I could properly accept the $10,000 award that went with it. I did not think I could publicly refuse the money; as George Washington once said of a gift of gratitude that a state legislature had offered him, to say no would be "too ostentatious a display of disinterestedness." I discussed the matter privately with Lynne Cheney, the director of the Endowment, and upon looking into it she learned that if I simply refused the stipend I would still have to pay federal income taxes on it. What we finally hit upon was that I would formally, but without publicity, donate the lecture. The address itself is republished in the appendix to this volume. (It ultimately leaked out that I had received no money for the performance, though not until after a *New York Times* reporter tut-tutted me for being critical of an agency but taking its money all the while.)

Nonetheless, I took home beaucoup loot from the bicentennial, for the invitations poured in. The honorarium for the first lectures I gave was $1,500, but I rapidly upped that in increments of $500 until I settled on a standard fee of $3,000. I don't recall how many speeches I gave, but a couple of clues will provide an idea. For nearly two years I spoke somewhere in the country—usually at universities—at least twice a month. We kept count of the invitations I turned down but quit counting when the number reached a hundred. On one occasion I lectured at William and Mary, West Point, Cornell, and Dartmouth on a single looping trip. We earned enough to pay off the mortgage, buy each of us a car, and buy me a pickup truck and a tractor.

With rare exceptions, the audiences were enthusiastic. My favorite was at West Point: the students there are clean-cut, wholesome kids who somehow look alike irrespective of race or sex. My least favorite was a southern university that will remain nameless, whose faculty was populated by liberal Ivy League Ph.D.s who were ashamed to be in the deep South and who infected their students with their own discontents. Otherwise, the receptions were won-

September 1986 to December 1987: Forrest gives one of his many
bicentennial lectures

derfully warm. Part of the reason was technique. Writing for the ear
is different from writing for the eye, and I have worked long and
hard at it. I have also learned to alleviate attention-span difficulties—
which necessarily arise when one reads a paper running forty-five
minutes to a group accustomed to sixty-second sound bites and fre-
quent commercial breaks—by making marginal notes every few
pages for ad libbing an anecdote or a witty aside. But the main reason for the favorable responses was that the audiences craved to
hear the message I delivered. In the speeches I blended realism, paint-
ing the Founders as the flawed human beings they were, with a
wholesome appreciation for the veritable miracle they wrought.
When one realizes that Gouverneur Morris, who actually wrote the
finished Constitution, was an inveterate woman chaser; that Alexander Hamilton, who gave it life, was exceedingly vain and an adul-

terer to boot; that George Washington, without whom it would have been impossible, had a violent temper, was addicted to gambling, and was "a most horrid swearer"; when one realizes these things, one is all the more thrilled by, and grateful for, what they bequeathed to us. (I should add that I expected to be given just one invitation to speak during the celebration of the bicentennial of the Bill of Rights, for I agree with Hamilton that the Bill of Rights was unnecessary and pernicious. I was right: I presented a paper saying that and was not invited to give another.)

As for productive research and writing, I did precious little during that period, though various pieces were collected and published by the University Press of Kansas as a little volume, *Requiem: Variations on Eighteenth-Century Themes* (1988). The dry spell—my next major book did not appear until the mid-1990s—was prolonged by a misadventure. At some point I decided that I wanted to undertake a history of international law, from the *jus gentium* of the Romans to the evolution of positive international law in the form of treaties. The project seemed reasonable, for the literature on the subject during the ancient and medieval periods was abundant, and I had in the course of doing the Hamilton biography read the works of the great theorists of the law of nations: Grotius, Burlamaqui, and Vattel. The endeavor, however, was foolhardy, and after spending two or three years making notes cast in a narrative and analytical form, I had six chapters and perhaps 300 pages. Then I dropped the subject.

I did publish two more books with the University Press of Kansas before starting the present one. The first was *The American Presidency: An Intellectual History* (1994). I began thinking about the presidency as an institution in the wake of the election of Jimmy Carter, when I wrote an article for *Commentary* called "A Mirror for Presidents." In it, I formulated the proposition that the office of president is dual in nature, one function being to run the executive branch, the other being ritualistic and ceremonial—serving as a surrogate king, to fulfill what I regard as an inborn (if not speakable)

October 1989: At a barbeque at the McClenden Ranch in Dallas as part of the regional meeting of the Philadelphia Society; Forrest was president of the Society at that time

October 1992: At a private dinner with President Nixon at his residence in New Jersey

craving for a monarch. My store of knowledge on the subject derived from my books on Washington and Jefferson as well as from reading a number of the books in the Kansas presidency series. My curiosity was whetted by a couple of things. I noticed a shift in attitudes toward the presidency on the part of liberals and conservatives: liberals had long advocated a strong presidency, conservatives a weak one, and by the mid-1980s the positions were reversed. The other was that I met and had conversations with two presidents, Ronald Reagan and Richard Nixon. With Reagan, the conversation was at a White House reception he gave for me on the occasion of the Jefferson Lecture. With Nixon, the discussion took place at dinner in his New Jersey apartment in 1992. (He was awesomely learned about history; it was rather like spending an evening with, say, John Adams.)

The American Presidency concludes after 480 pages that "though the powers of the office have sometimes been grossly abused, though the presidency has become almost impossible to manage, and though the caliber of the people who have served as chief executive has de-clined erratically but persistently from the day George Washington left office," the institution has been "unparalleled in its stability" and "has been responsible for less harm and more good, in the nation and in the world, than perhaps any other secular institution in history."

The second book was *States' Rights and the Union: Imperium in Imperio, 1776–1876* (2000). Poking around into the subject, I was surprised to learn that, central as the idea of states' rights has been in American history, nobody had done a book-length study of the subject. Accordingly, I set out to do one myself. The essential points I made were that the advocates of the doctrine were justified by the history of the Founding and that the position was held not only by John C. Calhoun and various southern spokesmen but also, and as frequently, by northerners when they were displeased by the activi-ties of the federal government.

The book as published is just half the length I originally planned. I had intended to carry the subject to recent times, which would have involved a long book indeed. But while I was working on it I had oc-casion to review a book by Michael F. Holt called *The Rise and Fall of the American Whig Party: Jacksonian Politics and the Onset of the Civil War,* which runs to more than 1,200 pages. In the review I pointed out that historians justify their existence by generalizing, by studying trees and describing forests, but what Holt had done was "study trees and describe leaves and branches." This unconscionably long and arid tome deterred me from inflicting anything near that length upon my readers; so I ended the substantive part of my book in 1876 and added a brief concluding essay bringing the subject for-ward to the 1990s.

Meanwhile, in the real world, historical consciousness and knowl-edge among the generality of the American population had declined appallingly, and the quality of work being done by widely publicized historians had declined even more so. In the spring of 1986, a study of American students revealed that in a multiple-choice test, 68 percent of them "were unable to place the Civil War in the correct half-century, 1850–1900." In February of 2000, the American Council of Trustees and Alumni released the results of a study of seniors in the fifty-five most prestigious universities (as ranked by *U.S. News & World Report*) showing that 81 percent of them had failed a history test given to high school students by the National Association of Educational Progress.[8]

In the wake of the 1986 tests came an episode that demonstrated the extent of the profession's degeneration. Lynne Cheney was disturbed by the test's findings and, acting through the Endowment, funded a National Center for History in the Schools and entrusted it with the task of producing a volume of *National Standards for United States History* and a companion volume, *National Standards for World History*. Unbeknownst to Dr. Cheney, radicals had long since undertaken a Maoist "march through the institutions" and had captured the American Historical Association and the Organization of American Historians. A chief director of the *National Standards* project was Gary B. Nash, who was soon to become president of the American Historical Association.[9]

The volumes, each running about 300 pages, were published in 1994, and Cheney was aghast. She wrote an article for the *Wall Street Journal* repudiating them for their "politically correct" biases; for the inordinate amount of space they devoted to the contributions of Indians, blacks, and women; and for their endless dwelling on the darker side of the American past, including McCarthyism and the Ku Klux Klan. Moreover, the American volume made little or no mention of George Washington, Daniel Webster, Thomas Edison, or the Wright brothers, to name but a few.[10]

8. Wilcomb Washburn, "Serious Questions about the *National Standards for United States History*," *Continuity: A Journal of History* 19 (Spring 1995): 47; Gary Palmer, "Teaching History is Important to Future of U.S.," *Tuscaloosa News*, September 15, 2002, 6D.

9. "Introduction," *Continuity* 19 (Spring 1995): 1–3.

10. Ibid.

December 11, 2003: Dinner with President and Mrs. Bush at the White House

Others joined in the criticism. Wilcomb Washburn pointed out that in discussing World War II, the *National Standards* made virtually no references to battles and campaigns but glorified minority contributions and dwelt excessively on such matters as the internment of Japanese Americans. He also noted, without mentioning William Appleman Williams by name, that Williams' version of the origins of the Cold War was endorsed in the *Standards*. Herman Belz quoted a passage on the Civil War indicating that "students have many opportunities to study heroism and cowardice, triumph and tragedy, and hardship, pain, grief and death wrought by conflict." The next sentence, however, trivializes the subject by announcing that "another important topic is how the war necessarily obliged both northern and southern women to adapt to new and unsettling conditions." Burton W. Folsom took the *Standards* to task for failing to describe the origins of the constitutional system, for being biased against capitalism, for neglecting to give an account of how the American economy grew at such an astonishing rate, and for being devoid of balance. In the section on the Civil War, for example, Harriet Tubman is mentioned six times, whereas Lincoln's Gettysburg Address and Ulysses S. Grant are each mentioned once, and Robert E. Lee does not appear at all.[11]

I read the *National Standards* too and published a small critique. I pointed out that when the *Standards* deigned to treat mainstream American history in a nondisparaging way, it teemed with factual errors. In the sections that dealt with my particular area of expertise, from the Revolution to 1815, the level of ignorance was high. On page 70 alone, introducing "Era 3: Revolution and the New Nation," I detected nine major errors of fact, plus a complete lack of comprehension of the period and no familiarity with modern scholarship. I added that even had the execution been able and fair, the notion of a uniform set of history standards smacked of the kind of thought control described by George Orwell in his nightmarish futuristic novel *1984*.[12]

Nash admitted that the work had shortcomings, made a half-hearted effort to defend the project, and actually published a revised edition two years later, but it never caught on. What is more important, however, is that many professional historians taught along the lines of the *Standards* anyway. To show the lack of balance in the profession, Washburn cited "a 1975 study by Everett C. Ladd and Seymour Martin Lipset . . . which found only a tiny percentage of professors in major universities regularly voting Republican," and a 1995 study of the political affiliations of the faculty at Stanford

11. Washburn, "Serious Questions," Herman Belz, "National Standards for United States History: The Limits of Liberal Orthodoxy," and Burton W. Folsom, Jr., "Three Arguments against the *National Standards for United States History*," *Continuity* 19 (Spring 1995): 54, 62, 73–78.

12. Forrest McDonald, "National Standards for United States History: An Idea Whose Time Should Never Come," *Continuity* 19 (Spring 1995): 41–45.

showing that in the history department twenty-two members identified themselves as Democrats, two as Republicans.[13]

And the situation worsened: around the turn of the twenty-first century, if not before, the profession came to be plagued by outright dishonesty. I say "if not before," for I know of an instance in the 1960s
in which a person received a Ph.D. from an Ivy League institution
for a dissertation that was made up out of the whole cloth, including an elaborate and extensive set of footnote references to nonexistent manuscripts in the Library of Congress. The dissertation
was later published by a reputable university press. After the fraud
was uncovered, the press recalled copies of the book. But I believe
that sort of thing has been extremely rare. What began to appear
around the year 2000 reached epidemic proportions.

One scandal was a more or less harmless deception by a professor of history at Mount Holyoke named Joseph Ellis. Ellis was a reputable scholar, the author of half a dozen well-received books,
mainly about eighteenth-century Americans. However, he had for
years told his students, his colleagues, and fellow historians that he
was a veteran of combat in the Vietnam War, and he embellished his
story with vivid accounts of supposed combat experiences. Somehow it came to light that he had made up the whole thing and had
never actually been in Vietnam. The matter was widely publicized,
and an embarrassed Mount Holyoke administration reprimanded
him and took away his endowed chair.

No one charged that his fantasizing spilled into his scholarship.
I read his *Founding Brothers,* and though it is marked by a number
of minor errors of fact and transcription, is sometimes repetitive,
and is shallow in its reading of a few characters (especially Alexander Hamilton), it is an honest work and contains nothing fictitious.
Indeed, its interpretation of Thomas Jefferson is quite perceptive.

13. Washburn, "Serious Questions," 51. For an article indicating that the essence
of the *Standards* is being taught in New Jersey, see Adam Scrupski, "American History Lessons in New Jersey," *Academic Questions* 15 (Summer 2002): 62–76.

The only harm done by the revelation of Ellis' fantasy life was to give the profession a black eye.[14]

More harm followed in a succession of plagiarism charges against historians. Some charges involved lesser lights in the profession, but the publicity attending them stimulated reporters to dig up plagiarism charges against better-known scholars, most notably Lyndon Johnson's biographer and presidential historian Doris Kearns Goodwin and the best-selling biographer of Eisenhower and Nixon, Stephen Ambrose. Goodwin admitted the charges; Ambrose demurred. Then in early 2003 the *New York Times* (soon to suffer its own scandals) reported that a historian at the United States Naval Academy, Brian VanDeMark, had included more than thirty passages in *Pandora's Keepers: Nine Men and the Atomic Bomb* that were "identical or almost identical to work in four books by other historians." VanDeMark defended a few of the passages as "reasonable paraphrases" but admitted that the rest would have to be "reworded or credited in a footnote."[15]

The VanDeMark case triggered a change in policy regarding plagiarism charges by the American Historical Association. Since 1988, the procedure in such matters had been to appoint six members to study the accusations in secret, hear charges and defenses, examine the evidence, and after many months report the findings to the association. The process was "cumbersome" and, said the association's executive director, required "significant resources that we don't have." The revised policy was to investigate charges openly so as to expedite hearings and "to educate historians, students and the public."[16]

Even as the plagiarism issue was raising questions about the integrity and ethical standards of the historical profession, a far graver

14. Joseph Ellis, *Founding Brothers: The Revolutionary Generation* (New York, 2000).

15. "Historians' Group Changes Policy on Plagiarism," *Tuscaloosa News,* June 1, 2003, 5A; Philip Terzian, "Ambrose's Slip Tarnishes Literary Reputation," *Richmond Times-Dispatch*, February 3, 2002, F5.

16. "Historians' Group Changes Policy on Plagiarism," *Tuscaloosa News,* June 1, 2003, 5A.

scandal was coming to light, and the way it unfolded tarnished the reputations of some of the country's foremost practitioners of history. In September of 2000, a history professor at Emory University, Michael Bellesiles, published *Arming America: The Origins of a National Gun Culture.* In it he wrote that "the power of image and myth repeatedly overwhelms reality in discussions of early American firearms." Claiming to have examined 11,170 probate records—documents inventorying the property holdings of people at the time of their deaths—he asserted that "America's gun culture is an invented tradition" and that only a small fraction of Americans owned guns during the eighteenth and nineteenth centuries.[17]

Arming America received an enthusiastic welcome from the left-leaning historians who dominate the profession, for its strong implication was that, in context, the Second Amendment protected group rights to bear arms, not individual rights, and the vast majority of historians favor strict gun-control legislation. Bellesiles had published an article on the subject in the *Journal of American History* in 1996, and it won an award as "Best Article of the Year." The book was praised in the *Washington Post* and no less a man than Edmund Morgan raved about it in the *New York Review of Books,* saying "the evidence is overwhelming. First of all are the Probate Records." Other reviewers stressed the importance of Bellesiles' use of the probate records. Columbia University voted to award the book the Bancroft Prize. The decision was applauded, and the kudos continued to pour in.[18]

Something fishy cropped up at the outset, however, and things grew fishier as time went by. James Lindgren, a law professor at Northwestern, was engaged in research on a related subject, and he sent Bellesiles an e-mail requesting information about the location of records he had cited. Bellesiles replied that he had read them on

17. Melissa Seckora, "Disarming America," *National Review,* October 15, 2001, 50–54; Kimberly A. Strassel, "Guns and Poses," *Wall Street Journal,* February 22, 2002, op-ed page.

18. Seckora, "Disarming America," 50.

microfilm at a branch of the United States Archives in East Point, Georgia. On inquiring there, Lindgren was informed the archive had no such records. Faced with that fact, Bellesiles said he had consulted the records in about thirty different repositories around the country but could not send details because his notes had been damaged by a flood.[19]

Next, Lindgren and an associate, Justin Heather, checked a set of probate records for Providence, Rhode Island, that Bellesiles had cited and found that the records showed a far higher distribution of gun ownership than Bellesiles had reported. Something similar happened in regard to records in Vermont, where Heather found that 40 percent of the households had guns, whereas Bellesiles had reported that 15 percent did. A reporter for the *Boston Globe* duplicated the check, with similar results. Confronted with the *Globe*'s story, Bellesiles claimed "somebody had hacked into his Web site and changed his data."[20]

Bellesiles also claimed that he had consulted probate records for people who died in 1849–1850 and 1858–1859 in San Francisco, but as it turned out, those records had been destroyed in the San Francisco earthquake and fire in 1906. Bellesiles suggested two other places where he might have used the records, but they proved not to be there, either. Joyce Malcolm, a history professor at Bentley College, reported, "if you check his footnotes . . . it is not just an odd mistake or a difference of interpretation, but misrepresentation of what his sources [if they exist] actually say, time after time after time." Finally, the *William and Mary Quarterly* asked four scholars to evaluate *Arming America*. Three of them roundly condemned the book; the fourth, Jack Rakove, hedged.[21]

The upshot was that Bellesiles resigned from Emory in disgrace in October of 2002, still insisting that the book was "fundamentally

19. Strassel, "Guns and Poses."
20. Ibid.
21. Seckora, "Disarming America," 53; Kimberley A. Strassel, "A Gun Battle Is Over: Truth Wins," *Wall Street Journal*, November 1, 2002.

sound," and Columbia took the unprecedented step of rescinding his Bancroft Prize and asking him to return the $4,000 in prize money.[22]

One would suppose that after such scandals the book-buying American public would be skeptical of anything turned out by a professional historian, and even suspect that the profession might be on its last legs.

My intention, when I got to this point, was to cite the reasons why I remain optimistic despite these troubles. I would have said something about how many serious works in history appear on the bestseller lists despite the scandals. I would have described how, the lunacy to the contrary notwithstanding, we have continued to make progress in field after field—in western history, for example, where historians have risen above victimology to a fresh, sophisticated understanding, or the Progressive period, in which interest in ethnicity has led to enriched interpretations replacing the older class-struggle view. I would have pointed to the emergence of a professional organization, the Historical Society, dedicated to promoting history of the kind we strove for before the advent of the New Left. I would have commented upon the enormous wealth of source material made readily available by modern technology.[23]

But when I confided this plan to Ellen, she said, "You can't do that. This is a book about history, and you would be talking about current events and forecasting the future." And she is right. The events I have just been describing happened, and they happened in the past, but in a past so recent that they do not yet qualify as history.

How much time must elapse before historical perspective can be brought to bear is not a matter of exactitude, but rules of thumb

22. "Prize for Book on Guns Rescinded," *Tuscaloosa News*, December 14, 2002.

23. See, for example, Richard W. Etulain, "The American West and Its Historians," *Historically Speaking* (June 2002): 15–17. The Bushes and the NEH have started a three-year "We the People" program to encourage the teaching of history; see Richard Brookhiser, "Lost in the Mists of Time," *Wall Street Journal*, June 13, 2003, W19.

apply. Generally speaking, we usually think that at least a generation is necessary, but *generation* is a nebulous term. Twenty or thirty
years is commonly regarded as the norm, but it can vary in accordance with one's age and memory. To college students today, the
presidency of Ronald Reagan is history, because it started before
they were born and ended before they were politically conscious. To
me, anything that happened after my thirtieth birthday, which was
in 1957, I regard as virtually current events.

A more important consideration is that enough time must elapse
so that one can know pretty much how things turned out. In one
sense, the ultimate outcome of events is unknowable, for anything
of consequence keeps on having consequences. That George Washington was in command of the American forces during the Revolution, for example, continues to have an impact on our lives today.
In another sense, Washington's effect on the British Empire and the
establishment of the American Republic was visible and could be
placed in historical perspective by the time he died in 1799—but
could not have been when he laid down his command in 1783, for
chapters in the story were yet to come. For such reasons as these, I
bow to my wife's judgment and decline to make the prognostications
that I had intended to make about the profession.

Instead, let me simply assert my optimism about history and the
history profession. That optimism may just be a reflection of my
psyche. I am a natural-born Pollyanna, constitutionally disposed toward optimism.[24] And though it may be my genetic programming
that makes me that way, a philosophy in the form of an attitude

24. In 1960 I gave a speech for Pembroke's freshman orientation; Ellen, a sixteen-
year-old freshman, was in the audience. As I later learned, Ellen determined on the
spot that she was going to marry me. I gave the same speech in Chicago in November 1990 on the occasion of receiving the Ingersoll Foundation's Richard M. Weaver
Award for Scholarly Letters, and the speech was published in *Chronicles* (February
1991). I delivered it a third time on my last day of classes before I retired. Thus it
constituted the first and last time that Ellen heard me address a group of students.
What follows is the conclusion of that speech.

toward life underlies it. I can describe that attitude no better than by saying that one has a duty to be grateful and joyful in the very fact of one's existence, and in the existence of one's fellow human beings. The cynic responds, why should one be joyful in life, when in no time it is followed by death, and when with each person's death the whole universe, for that person, ceases to exist? My answer strikes me as reasonable, though perhaps it is merely a rationalization of my own joy. Scientists, as we know, deal in probabilities rather than, as was once thought, in absolute laws. Anything that happens with a probability of, say, ten to the millionth power to one, is pretty much a sure thing. If Darwin's theory of evolution has validity, what do you suppose the probability of man's existence is? I am speaking of the movement up through the countless environmental changes and mutations necessary for the evolution from primordial ooze to humanity. I can assure you that it is considerably more far-fetched than a ten-to-the-millionth-power-to-one shot; it is approximately as likely as the spontaneous transformation of this book into an atom of plutonium.[25]

And given the existence of human beings, the probabilities against my own existence—or yours—are again as high as those against the existence of man. You can attribute this to God, or to big bangs, or to sheer blind luck; all I can do is shout hallelujah, I got here! My God, I got here! In the face of this colossal fact, I must exult in my gratitude, for everything else is trivial: no matter what the uncertainties, whether things are better or worse, whether I am hungry or well fed, whether I am sick or healthy, or cold or comfortable, or honored and respected or despised and kicked and beaten, even that I shall soon be leaving, all is trivial compared to the fact that I got here. I am a miracle, and so, dear reader, are you. Let us rejoice together.

25. In Francis J. Beckwith, "Science and Religion Twenty Years after *McLean* v. *Arkansas:* Evolution, Public Education, and the New Challenge of Intelligent Design," *Harvard Journal of Law & Public Policy* 26 (Spring 2003): 482, the author quotes Hugh Ross, "Big Bang Model Refined by Fire," that there is "much less than 1 chance in one hundred billion trillion trillion trillion [that there] exists . . . even one" site in the universe where life "would occur."

APPENDIX

■

The Intellectual World of
the Founding Fathers

Various intellectuals have suggested that the best thing Americans could do to commemorate the two-hundredth anniversary of our Constitution would be to rewrite it to reflect the realities of the twentieth century. Various jurists have suggested that the Supreme Court is, and should be, doing just that. The assumption underlying both notions is that our pool of knowledge and understanding about human nature and political institutions is far more sophisticated than any that could have been available in the simple frontier society of eighteenth-century America.

That assumption is as presumptuous as it is uninformed. To put it bluntly, it would be impossible in America today to assemble a group of people with anything near the combined experience, learning, and wisdom that the fifty-five authors of the Constitution took with them to Philadelphia in the summer of 1787. As an appetizer, I offer a couple of corroborative tidbits. Thirty-five of the delegates had attended college. Just to enter college during the eighteenth

Forrest and Ellen S. McDonald, *Requiem: Variation on Eighteenth-Century Themes* (Lawrence: University Press of Kansas, 1988), 1–22.

century—which students normally did at the age of fourteen or fifteen—it was necessary, among other things, to be able to read and
translate from the original Latin into English (I quote from the requirements at King's College—now Columbia—which were typical)
"the first three of Tully's Select Orations and the first three books
of Virgil's Aeneid" and to translate the first ten chapters of the
Gospel of John from Greek into Latin, as well as to be "expert in
arithmetic" and to have a "blameless moral character." I ask you,
how many Americans today could even get into college, given those
requirements?

Moreover, though the Framers were, as Thomas Jefferson called
them, a group of demigods, it would have been easy in America in
1787 to have assembled another five, possibly ten, constitutional
conventions that would have matched the actual convention in every
way except for the incomparable luster of George Washington. After
all, neither Jefferson nor John Adams was in the Great Convention,
nor were John Hancock, Noah Webster, Richard Henry Lee, Samuel
Adams, David Rittenhouse, Benjamin Rush, Fisher Ames, John Taylor, and John Jay. Indeed, the state convention that ratified the Constitution in Virginia in 1788 included among its members, not counting the five who had sat in the Philadelphia Convention, John
Marshall, Patrick Henry, Edmund Pendleton, Light-Horse Harry
Lee, Bushrod Washington, William Grayson, and James Monroe,
along with thirty or forty less prominent but no less able men.

In fine, the formation of the republic was a product of America's
Golden Age, the likes of which we shall not see again.

The roots of America's eighteenth-century flowering are to be found
in part in the interplay between the physical environment and the
cultural and institutional baggage that immigrants from the British
Isles had brought with them to the New World. Nature's bounty was
rich in the areas settled by the British, though scarcely richer than in
those settled by the French and the Spanish. But whereas the French

kept their colonies under rigid political control from Paris and the Spanish transplanted entire institutional superstructures in their colonies, the British suffered theirs to develop for more than a century and a half under what has been called salutary neglect.

As a consequence, British-Americans could pick and choose among the institutions of the mother country, adapting those that were useful and casting off the rest. Among those that were never successfully planted in America were Britain's hereditary class structure; the bishopric and, except on a local basis, mandatory religious conformity; an economic order in which upward mobility was difficult at best and impossible for most; and a Parliament whose power was theoretically unlimited. Among the English institutions and attitudes that were firmly planted in America were the traditional idea that government must be lawful; the common law, which was adopted selectively, colony by colony; the practice of settling disputes through juries; reliance upon militias of armed citizens for defense and for the preservation of order; and the belief that the ownership of land, or the possession of enough other property to ensure an independent livelihood, was a prerequisite to the full rights and duties of citizenship. These, together with the development of such indigenous creations as the town meeting and such virtually indigenous practices as the responsibility of church ministers to their congregations, as well as the ready availability of land, bred a citizenry that was at once self-reliant and interdependent. What is more, the scheme of things required widespread participation in public affairs through face-to-face mechanisms, largely outside the framework of formal government. The daily business of life thus schooled Americans for responsible citizenship and for statesmanship.

Next in importance was that Americans were literate. Precisely what the literacy rate was cannot be determined: even to talk about "rates" is misleading, for they were literate but not numerate, which is to say that they had not fallen victim to the modern delusion that quality can be measured in numbers. It is clear, however, that thanks to the public school systems in the North and the proliferation of private academies and Scottish tutors in the South, a greater percentage of citizens could read and write than was true of any other nation on earth (and, I have no doubt, a greater percentage than can do so today). Furthermore, Americans who had had any schooling at all had been exposed to eight- and ten-hour days of drilling, at the hands of stern taskmasters, in Latin and Greek. This was designed to build character, discipline the mind, and instill moral principles, in addition to teaching language skills. (Educated French military officers who served in the United States during the Revolution found that even when they knew no English and Americans knew no French, they could converse with ordinary Americans in Latin.)

Some indication of what reading meant to Americans can be seen by reference to the newspapers of the day. Nearly four times as many newspapers were published in the United States as were published in France, though France had six times as many people and was possibly the most literate nation on the European continent. American papers rarely carried local news, on the assumption that everybody knew what was happening locally; instead, they reported what was taking place in other states and nations. Into New York and Philadelphia alone, 2,000 ships arrived each year, bearing information as well as goods from all parts of the Atlantic world, and that information was routinely recorded in the newspapers, so that ordinary farmers and shop-keepers and craftsmen were kept abreast of affairs from Vienna to Venezuela, from Madrid to Moscow, from London and Paris to Martinique and Jamaica.

And the readers were sophisticated as well as cosmopolitan. Let us recall that the *Federalist* essays—the classic analysis of the Constitution and one of the most profound treatises on political theory ever penned—were originally published as a series of articles in a New York newspaper and were so popular that they were reprinted in other papers throughout the country. Moreover, Alexander Hamilton, James Madison, and John Jay, in signing the essays with the pseudonym Publius, could assume that readers would know that they were identifying themselves with the ancient Roman who, following Lucius Brutus's overthrow of the last king of Rome, had established the republican foundation of the Roman government. Let me offer a somewhat more esoteric example. In 1786 Isaiah Thomas, printer of a weekly newspaper in Worcester, Massachusetts, called the *Massachusetts Spy,* was seeking ways to amuse his readers in the absence of pressing news. There had been some controversy over Alexander Pope's translation of the *Iliad*—Samuel Johnson is said to have quipped, "It is beautiful, sir, but is it Homer?"—and Thomas gave his readers the opportunity to decide for themselves by printing Pope's translation and the original Greek in parallel columns.

Complementing the habit of reading was the leisurely pace of life, which gave Americans time to reflect upon and discuss what they read. This is an important point to understand. In our modern era of instantaneous communication, we are so continuously bombarded with sights and sounds and information that to retain our sanity, we have to develop ways of filtering out or ignoring the bewildering array of attacks upon our senses. Many of you are aware of the study showing that the average congressman has something in the order of twelve minutes a day to be alone and think. It was quite otherwise in the eighteenth century. There was no need to hurry in a world in which exchanging letters between Philadelphia and London took twelve weeks, and between Boston and Savannah four to six weeks. Besides, Americans had access to only a limited number of books—the library that was available to the Framers, one of the nation's largest, the Library Company of Philadelphia, contained 5,000 volumes—and thus one could read them again and again, savor them and brood over them, and absorb even the most profound and abstruse of them wholly into one's being.

The content of the reading, cushioning as it did Americans' perceptions of the monumental events of the Revolutionary epoch, also helped make the founding generation such a remarkable lot of men.

Contrary to a persistent notion, Americans were all but untouched by the writers of the French Enlightenment, unless Montesquieu be so considered (they did read Montesquieu, though I suspect only selectively). Some exotic and omnivorous readers, Benjamin Rush for instance, did read Rousseau, and many had at least heard of Voltaire and Diderot. But Americans by and large did not read the philosophes, in no small measure for the reason that Americans were immune to the antireligious virus that had infected the French.

Instead, all public men could be expected to be versed in a half-dozen general categories of writings in addition, of course, to the Holy Bible. They cited the Bible more than any other source, and unsurprisingly, the most cited book of the Bible was Deuteronomy. Of the secular categories, the first was also law, including both what was called "natural law" and the laws of England. The foremost treatises on natural law were those of the Genevan Jean Jacques Burlamaqui and his greatest pupil, Emmerich de Vattel; natural-law principles, at least in theory, governed the conduct of international relations, including the rules of war. Readers could in fact become familiar with Burlamaqui's thinking as they studied English law, for it is summarized in the first volume of Sir William Blackstone's *Commentaries on the Laws of England,* a work that, according to Madison, was "in every man's hand." Madison doubtless overstated, but there were considerably more copies of Blackstone sold in America than there were lawyers, and Blackstone was the second most frequently cited author in all the American political literature from the 1760s through the 1780s.

Another category was the ancient classics. Among the widely read Romans were Cicero, Tacitus, and Sallust; among the Greeks, Demosthenes, Aristotle, and Polybius. By far the most generally read book, however, was Plutarch's *Lives of the Noble Grecians and Romans,* in John Dryden's translation. It should be noted that few Americans appreciated Plato. To John Adams, Jefferson described Plato's *Republic* as a mass of "whimsies . . . puerilities and unintelligible jargon." Adams facetiously replied that the only two things he had learned from Plato were a cure for the hiccups and whence Ben Franklin had plagiarized some of his ideas.

From the classical authors and from Blackstone, Americans derived an understanding of history and a profound respect for its value; but from other writers they also learned a peculiar version of history that became a fundamental part of their worldview and, indeed, an enduring feature of American political discourse. This was the so-called Whig interpretation of history, which they learned from, among others, John Trenchard, Thomas Gordon, and Viscount Bolingbroke: the Whig version taught that history was an endless alternation between conspiracies by a few wicked and designing men to destroy popular liberties and the discovery and frustration of those plots by champions of the people. In accordance with that perception, American Patriots "discovered" during the 1760s and 1770s that a sinister combination of money men and ministers of the Crown was plotting to enslave them; and during the 1780s and 1790s a succession of equally monstrous plots was denounced by one political group or another. Nor did it stop there: Andrew Jackson and his followers discovered the Monster Banking Monopoly; the Populists discovered Wall Street and the Gold Conspiracy; and in the twentieth century, we have had the Trusts, the Malefactors of Great Wealth, the Military-Industrial Complex, and the Imperial Presidency.

Yet another body of literature studied by public men was that concerning "political economy," the newly devised "science" that began to emerge when men started to realize that economic activity need not be a zero-sum game and that governmental policies might profoundly influence the growth or decline of the wealth of nations. A number of writers treated the subject, but only three, all Scots, reached sizable audiences in America: Sir James Steuart, an advocate of a managed economy whose work had a powerful impact upon Hamilton, and David Hume and Adam Smith, advocates of a free-market economy who were most appreciated south of the Mason-Dixon line.

Finally, there were works that bore directly upon the task of erecting institutions to preserve free government, namely, treatises on political theory and upon the nature of man and society. Obviously the ancients, along with Bolingbroke, Montesquieu, and Blackstone, had a great deal to offer. Another potent influence was John Locke, whose *Second Treatise of Civil Government* provided the theoretical underpinnings for the Declaration of Independence and whose *Essay Concerning Human Understanding* was even more widely read. In addition, there were the Scottish Common Sense philosophers, who held that all men are equally endowed with a moral sense—that is, an inborn sense of what is right and what is wrong, of what is good and what is evil—with a disposition to do good, and with equal capacities to judge whether their rulers are good or bad. It was but a short step from that position to radical democracy, and it was no step at all to the conclusion that slavery is evil. A considerably different, though not opposite, view was that of Hume and Smith, whose theory of moral sentiments held that men are inspired to do good by peer pressure rather than by the voice of conscience.

Before turning to the practical applications the Framers made of all this—and they insisted that they were interested solely in "useful" knowledge, not what was merely ornamental, speculative, or abstract—I should like to offer a couple of observations about what has been said so far. Those who are familiar with the literature will be aware that the lessons it taught were far from perfectly compatible, one with another. The Framers were quite aware of this but were not concerned by it. They were politically multilingual, able to speak in the diverse idioms of Locke, the classical republicans, Hume, and many others, depending upon what seemed rhetorically appropriate to the argument at hand. When the order of the day was loyal opposition to measures of Parliament, as it was during the 1760s and 1770s, Bolingbroke was suitable; when time came to break with the mother country, Bolingbroke was inadequate but Locke filled the bill; and upon the winning of independence, Locke became obsolete—because subversive. The inference to be drawn, clearly, is that the Framers, with some exceptions, were not ideologues, slavishly addicted to one political theory or another, but men who were accustomed to use political theorists to buttress positions that they adopted for experiential and prudential reasons.

My other somewhat digressive observation concerns those of the founding generation who did not do much reading. Among the Framers themselves, the obvious example is George Washington, who was not a bookish man; nor, as far as I can tell, were such other luminaries in the Constitutional Convention as Robert Morris, Nathaniel Gorham, and Roger Sherman. Moreover, large numbers of ordinary Americans rarely read anything but the Bible and the newspapers; the German traveler Johann David Schopf recorded that he met many people in Virginia who told him that a great man named Thomas Jefferson had written an important book, but he met none who could tell him what was in it. But one did not need to read extensively to become versed in the ideas of the various authors I have mentioned, for their ideas permeated the very air Americans breathed. In addition to the learned polemics that appeared regularly in newspapers, Americans imbibed large draughts of history and philosophy from plays—Washington was an inveterate theatergoer—and from oratory. Oratorical powers were especially respected and were genuine sources of popular entertainment, particularly adapted to commemorative occasions and to judges' charges to grand juries. Americans, who were connoisseurs as well as aficionados, could listen to good orators literally for hours on end. In one oration delivered on the eleventh anniversary of the Boston Massacre, for example, Thomas Dawes, Jr., harangued a large crowd with a learned history of republics in which he quoted, among others, Marcus Aurelius, Ovid, Pope, Seneca, Newton, Blair, Juvenal, Addison, Blackstone, and the Bible. Thus it was that Jefferson could honestly say, many years later, that he had written the Declaration of Independence without reference to any book, for the language of Locke's *Second Treatise* was common currency of the realm.

Let us now turn to the question of how the Framers applied what they knew and understood. Their aim was to secure liberty and justice—and for some, to attain greatness as a nation—through the instrumentality of a lawful and limited system of government. In the undertaking, they were guided by this principle: the extent to which limited government is feasible is determined by the extent to which the people, socially and individually, can govern themselves. I can put that more simply for the sake of emphasis: if citizens can behave themselves and make do for themselves, they need little government; if they cannot, they need a great deal of government. (Is it necessary to add the corollary, that the more government does for them, the less able they become to do for themselves?)

Americans were well endowed institutionally and experientially to manage the social aspects of self-government; but the matter of each individual's government of himself was more problematical. After a burst of naive enthusiasm in 1776, patriots—especially those who were actively engaged in the struggle for independence—rapidly ran out of faith in the civic virtue of the American people. Embezzlement, profiteering, trade with the enemy, and local jealousies plagued the public councils from the Continental Congress to the statehouses and infested private life from the merchants in their countinghouses to farmers in their fields.

The Framers could and did comprehend this triumph of self-interest over the public interest in terms of the prevailing understanding of the workings of the human psyche. That understanding was grounded in the theory that men are governed by their passions—not passions in the sense of violent emotions, but in the sense of drives for self-gratification, the seeking of pleasure and the avoidance of pain. Some passions, such as hunger and lust, grief and joy, hope and fear, were direct passions; others, such as pride and humility, love and hatred, were indirect; but either way, though this period of history is sometimes called the Age of Reason, it was generally believed that reason itself is rarely if ever a motive force. Rather, reason was regarded as a morally neutral instrument whose usual function was to serve the passions. It was also generally believed that every person had one ruling passion that tended to override the rest, and it was a cliché that the passions motivating most men in government were avarice and ambition, the love of money and the love of power. Accordingly, when Americans as individuals behaved badly, they were only following the dictates of human nature.

The theory of the passions would seem to have impaled the Framers upon a dilemma; but some few had contrived to escape its horns. For some, indeed, no contrivance was necessary. Men are driven by a variety of passions, many of which are noble: love of country, desire for glory, hunger for Fame (which was defined as immortality earned through the remembrance of a grateful posterity). When any noble passion becomes a man's ruling passion, which was true of a considerable number of the Framers, he must necessarily live his life in virtuous service to the public.

Whatever their passions, men could meliorate their baseness through religion, which nearly every American believed was a necessary, but which almost none believed was a sufficient, condition of morality. In an ultimate sense, moral accountability was to God; and that was no trivial abstraction in a society wherein belief in a future state of eternal rewards and punishments was nearly universal and wherein reminders of one's own mortality were almost continuous, since half the population died before coming of age. Moreover, American religion was Protestant, and even those few who professed themselves to be Deists or whose religious observances seemed to be *pro forma* consciously or unconsciously shared a Protestant Christian worldview. A telling example is seen in the Virginia Bill of Rights of 1776, which declared that "all men are equally entitled to the free exercise of religion, according to the dictates of their conscience," but went on to say that "it is the mutual duty of all to practice Christian forebearance, love, and charity towards each other." Similarly, the First Congress, which approved the religious-establishment clause of the First Amendment, also appointed a Protestant chaplain.

The common viewpoint was expressed by Richard Henry Lee when he said that "refiners may weave as fine a web of reason as they please, but the experience of all times shows Religion to be the guardian of morals," an attitude that Washington made explicit in his Farewell Address. Yet the Founders' religion itself, postulating as it did a Great Chain of Being in which men stand between the beasts and the angels, precluded the acceptance of any belief in the perfectibility of man; and it was that, man's sinful nature, which made religion insufficient to control men's behavior in this world.

There were, however, secular means of self-improvement, all of which, philosophically, rested on the premise that the social instinct is one of the primary passions governing mankind: the desire to have the approval, or at least to avoid the animosity, of one's peers ranks with the physical appetites as a motivating force in human affairs. It was in this other-directed spirit that the adolescent George Washington could record 110 "Rules of Civility and Decent Behaviour in Company and Conversation," rules that formed a manual of etiquette for circumstances ranging from being at the dinner table ("Being Set at meat Scratch not neither Spit Cough or blow your Nose except there's a Necessity for it") to being "In Company of those of Higher Quality than yourself" ("Speak not till you are ask'd a Question then Stand upright put off your Hat & Answer in a few words"). Nor was young Washington alone, as the enormous popularity of Lord Chesterfield's *Letters to His Son and Principles of Politeness* attests. Every kind of social interaction—from ballroom dancing to warfare, from forms of address to the complimentary closings of letters—became mannered, structured, and stylized. And thereby, through the studious cultivation of civilized behavior, the eighteenth century became the most civilized of all the ages. Every person learned the norms that attended his station, and anyone who violated those norms forfeited the esteem of his peers and betters.

How well such principles of etiquette led one to behave would vary, of course, with the quality of the persons whose approval one was seeking. Among the harshest criticisms leveled at Jefferson by his political enemies was that he courted "popular" favor, a charge that is mystifying until it is understood that "the populace" comprehended the vulgar herd and thus that a popular politician was a demagogue. Far better was it to disregard both popular favor and its opposite, the foolish advice that Polonius gave to Laertes, "to thine ownself be true," and instead to conduct one's self always with a view toward meriting the esteem of the wise and the just. And better yet, for public men, was it to seek the approval of posterity, of generations of discerning and virtuous people yet unborn.

One more means by which men could improve upon the baseness of their nature was through the concept of character. The term *character* was rarely used in the eighteenth century to refer to internal moral qualities. Rather, in its most general usage it referred to reputation: this man or that had a character for probity or fickleness or rashness. But it also, in polite society and among people in public life, meant a persona that one deliberately selected and always wore: one picked a role, like a part in a play, and contrived to act it unfailingly, ever to be in character. If one chose a character with which one was comfortable and if one played it long enough and consistently enough, by little and little it became a "second nature" that in practice superseded the first. One became what one pretended be.

The results, for good or ill, depended upon the character chosen and upon how well one acted it. Benjamin Franklin played a large and often contradictory array of characters during his long career, making it difficult for contemporaries and for historians to discern the true features of the man behind the masks. Jefferson essayed a succession of characters—he went so far as to change his handwriting several times—and though he played many of them with consummate skill, he never found a public character with which he was comfortable. When he retired from the presidency, he wrote to a friend, revealingly: "The whole of my life has been at war with my natural tastes, feelings and wishes. . . . Like a bow long bent I resume with delight the character and pursuits for which nature designed me." Washington, by contrast, played a progression of characters, each grander and nobler than the last, and played each so successfully that he ultimately transformed himself into a man of almost extrahuman virtue.

Not least among the advantages of role playing was that in America's open society, though not in Europe, it made possible aspiration to greatness, and it made greatness attainable. Where else and how else could an illegitimate orphan named Alexander Hamilton—the "bastard brat of a Scots pedlar," John Adams called him—aspire to and win military glory, then high social status, then exalted office, and in time, the immortal Fame of the Lawgiver, on the order of Solon and Lycurgus: one of those who, in Sir Francis Bacon's expression of Plutarch's conception, are "called *perpetui principes* or perpetual rulers, because they govern by their ordinances after they are gone."

Given everything I have said, one could imagine that the task of establishing an acceptable and durable frame of government would have posed few difficulties for the Founders. It might in fact have posed few difficulties, except that the Patriots of 1776, in their enthusiasm for defending American rights and in their revulsion against the supposed excesses of their king, committed the nation to two doctrines which, willy-nilly, ensnared the Americans in ideological thickets that were alien to their very being and contrary to their heritage, their experience, and their understanding of the nature of man. It took some time for the Framers to devise ways—and find the opportunity—to disentangle the nation from these snares.

The first of the doctrines was the natural-rights philosophy proclaimed in the Declaration of Independence. The Declaration asserted that all men are equally endowed by God with certain unalienable rights; that governments are instituted for the protection of those rights and derive their legitimate powers from the consent of the governed; and that if government becomes destructive of the ends for which it was established, the people reserve a right to alter or abolish it. Whatever the merits of these theories as philosophic abstractions, they are scarcely the stuff of which stable, lawful governments are made. As Blackstone put it, "No human laws will . . . suppose a case, which at once must destroy all law," nor will they make legal "provision for so desperate an event, as must render all legal provisions ineffectual."

Indeed, translated into the language of the multitude, the arguments of the Declaration could and did impede the winning of independence. The Massachusetts radical Benjamin Hichborn expressed a popular view when he declared, in an oration in Boston in 1777, that civil liberty was not a " 'government of laws,' made agreeable to charters, bills of rights or compacts, but a power existing in the people at large, at any time, for any cause, or for no cause, but their own sovereign pleasure, to alter or annihilate both the mode and essence of any . . . government." Acting on that understanding, farmers in the backcountry from New Hampshire to Georgia disrupted and hampered government throughout the war. Afterward, public men gradually stopped talking about the doctrines of the Declaration, allowing them to be muffled by a shroud of silence. Thus it was not by coincidence that the first edition of John Locke's *Two Treatises* to be published in America appeared in 1773 and that there was no subsequent American printing for 164 years; nor was it coincidental that after the Constitution had been adopted, the next favorable reference to the Declaration to appear in an official document in America was, as far as I am aware, in the South Carolina ordinance of secession in 1860.

Less easily escaped and more pernicious was an ideological commitment to republicanism. Although the United States more or less stumbled into republicanism by default—Americans had no hereditary aristocracy and had disowned their king—the "ism" comprehended a thoroughly developed system of political theory, drawn from the ancients and reformulated during the seventeenth and eighteenth centuries. It was synonymous neither with popular government nor with popular liberty, as is attested by the fact that it was embraced, at least in the abstract, by various petty "benevolent despots" among the German principalities and by no less grand a despot than Catherine the Great of Russia.

The vital—which is to say life-giving—principle of republics was *public virtue*. The word *virtue* in this phrase did not connote what is suggested by Christian virtue, with its emphasis upon humility and charity; nor did "the public" include everybody. Both *public* and *virtue* derive from Latin roots signifying manhood: the public included only free, independent adult males. Public virtue entailed discipline, strength, courage, endurance, industry, frugal living, and above all, unremitting devotion to the weal of the public's corporate self, the community of virtuous men. It was at once individualistic and communal: individualistic in that no person could be dependent upon another and still be counted as a member of the public, communal in that every man gave himself totally to the good of the public. Ultimately it was based upon the tradition of civic humanism, upon the Aristotelian notion that man is a political being whose highest form of self-realization can take place only through virtuous participation in public life. But the tradition of civic humanism, though meaningful to a goodly number of Americans—Hamilton and Madison, for instance—was foreign to the genius of the American people as a whole, who sought no salvation in politics. When they participated in government at all, they did so from a sense of duty (most commonly to help prevent government from encroaching upon their private lives), and when they returned to private station, they returned as Jefferson did, gladly and with a profound sense of relief.

Ideological republicanism was alien to Americans in other ways as well, for in addition to demanding eternal militance, it was both egalitarian (among those who qualified as part of the public) and totalitarian. As for the first, Montesquieu, who was regarded as the weightiest modern authority on the subject, insisted that virtue could be preserved only when the public was characterized by a "mediocrity" of "abilities and fortunes." Indeed, he wrote, if equality were to break down, "the republic will be utterly undone." Thus it was "absolutely necessary there should be some regulation in respect to . . . all . . . forms of contracting. For were we once allowed to dispose of our property to whom and how we pleased, the will of each individual would disturb the order of the fundamental law." And if that does not sound totalitarian enough, listen to the words of the New England republican Nathaniel Niles: "Every one must be required to do all he can that tends to the highest good of the state. . . . Every thing, however trifling, that tends, even in the lowest degree, to disserve the interest of the state must . . . be forbidden." These notions were scarcely compatible with Americans' conviction that government existed to protect people in their lives, liberties, and property or with their conception of liberty as security against arbitrary power.

Another part of the dogma wants notice: it was held that republics could be viable only in small territories and that if larger units were involved, they were best defended and held together through loose confederations. Hence the peculiar allocation of powers under the Articles of Confederation and the first state constitutions, whereby a unicameral Congress was given large responsibilities in international and interstate affairs but was given virtually no substantive powers for carrying out those responsibilities; and on the opposite side the several states were vested with almost unlimited powers. The bumbling and ineffectual way in which Congress managed is fairly well known.

What the real governments of the several United States were doing is less well known. They were oppressing American citizens under a burden of taxation and regulation greater than any they had ever experienced, greater than any that had been coveted by the wickedest minister who had ever advised the British Crown. The level of taxes during the 1780s was ten to twenty times prewar norms, and the increase in the volume of legislation, despite ostensible constitutional checks on the legislative power, dwarfed the increase in taxes. Quite in addition to the wholesale wartime persecutions of those who remained loyal to England, legislation was enacted to regulate what people could produce and sell and what they could charge for it; to interfere systematically with private commercial transactions and suspend the obligations of private contracts; to prohibit the purchase of luxuries, prescribe what people could eat and drink, and govern what they could wear; to regulate private morality, indoctrinate the citizens with official dogmas, and suppress contrary opinions; to inflate the currency deliberately to pay for the ever-mounting costs of government. All this and more was imposed upon a people so unaccustomed to taxation that they had been willing to rebel against their king rather than submit to even nominal taxes levied by Parliament; so unaccustomed to governmental intrusion upon their private lives as to be willing to fight and die to preserve their personal liberties; and so conservative that they could perceive the encroachments of Crown and Parliament only as violations of the ancient constitution. In sum, swept up by a temporary infatuation with ideological purity, Americans lost their moorings in history. And as is common in such circumstances, there arose an abundance of popular leaders to catch the winds of ideology in cynical pursuit of power and profit.

Thus it was that, though we usually think of the Constitution as having been designed to overcome the weaknesses of the Articles of Confederation by establishing new power, the vast majority of the Framers viewed the crisis of 1787 as having arisen from an excess of state government, a wanton and inept use of all governmental power, and a collapse of authority resulting from efforts to govern overmuch.

The members of the Great Convention sought to reestablish limits upon government and restore it to the rule of law. Fully 20 percent of the body of the Constitution is devoted to specifying things that government (state and/or federal) may not do. By contrast, only 11 percent of the text is concerned with positive grants of power. Of the powers granted, most were already vested in the old Confederation Congress; of the ten new powers, all had previously been exercised by the states. Consequently, the sum total of powers that could thenceforth be legitimately exercised was reduced, not enlarged. The main body of the Constitution—more than two-thirds of it—addresses the other part of the Framers' conception of their task, that of bringing government under the rule of law. The Constitution is primarily a structural and procedural document, specifying who is to exercise what powers and how. It is a body of law, designed to govern, not the people, but government itself; and it is written in language intelligible to all, that all might know whether it is being obeyed.

In devising these arrangements, the Framers were guided by principles but not by formulas. They aimed high, seeking, as Washington said, "a standard to which the wise and honest can repair"; but as Pierce Butler of South Carolina put it, they worked in the spirit of Solon, who gave the people of Athens, not the best government he could contrive in point of abstract political theory, but the best they would receive. Thus, rigid adherence to the doctrine of the separation of powers yielded to a system of checks and balances, and absolute dicta about the indivisibility of sovereignty were transmuted into a brilliant invention, federalism. The commitment to republicanism was similarly honored by instituting a form of government that redefined the term. Madison could now declare that a republic was a representative "government which derives all its powers directly or indirectly from the people" and in which no offices are hereditary; and as America flourished, *republic* would come to mean precisely what Madison said it meant.

And yet, even as the Framers were rejecting doctrine as formula, they faithfully adhered to the principle underlying Montesquieu's work—to its spirit. For Montesquieu's grand and abiding contribution to the science of politics was that no form or system of government is universally desirable or workable; instead, if government is to be viable, it must be made to conform to human nature and to the genius of the people—to their customs, morals, habits, institutions, aspirations. The Framers did just that, and thereby they used old materials to create a new order for the ages.

Let me end where I began, with those who would either new-model the Constitution through another convention or continue to stand idly by while government refashions it for us. I ask this: Are we better off, now that government at all levels is doing just what the Constitution was designed to prevent? And this: Has human nature changed so drastically, or has the genius of America? Was it folly or was it wisdom in the Framers to suppose that the people will govern themselves best if left to govern themselves? Was it folly or was it wisdom to maintain that there are limits upon what government can do and limits upon what it should attempt to do? Was it foolish or was it wise to insist that government by fiat is inherently oppressive, no matter how well intentioned its officers may be? These questions are of awesome portent, for the Framers legislated not only for themselves and their posterity but also, by example, for all mankind. As George Washington said in his Inaugural Address, "the sacred fire of liberty" is deeply and perhaps finally "staked upon the experiment entrusted to the hands of the American people." That fire was 3,000 years in the kindling. Let not our generation be the one to extinguish the flame.

Index

Abernethy, Thomas Perkins,
40, 404
Abraham, Nancy, 83
Adair, Douglass, 101–102,
108, 147
Adams, Henry, 37, 137
Adams, John, 16, 38, 168, 180
Adams, John Quincy, 38
Adams, Samuel, 168
Addison-Wesley, 109, 126
Alexandria Quartet, The, 6–8
Alien and Sedition Acts, 36
Ambition, 107, 108, 176–177
Ambrose, Stephen, 161
American Historical Association,
140, 141, 157, 161; presidents
of, 21–23, 25, 30, 87–88, 157
American Historical Review, 30,
105, 133
American History Research
Center, 74–77, 78, 79–85
Ames, Fisher, 168

Anti-Federalists, 33, 36, 68–69
Anti-Semitism, 91–92, 106–107
Appel, Livia, 69–70, 77
Aristocracy, 33, 169, 182
Army, U.S., 37, 44, 124
Articles of Confederation, 34,
108, 183–184
Atlanta, 56–57
Augustine, Saint, 26
Avarice, 73, 108, 176–177

Bacon, Sir Francis, 180
Bailyn, Bernard, 102
Bancroft, George, viii
Bancroft prize, 162, 164
Bank of the United States, 37;
Second Bank of the United
States, 37, 39, 98
Banks and Banking, 17, 37–39,
74, 84, 97–98, 109
Barker, Eugene Campbell, 20,
53–54, 55, 58

Banning, Lance, ix, 144
Barnes, Harry Elmer, 122
Baseball, 5–6, 50, 63–64, 87–88, 136
Bassett, John S., 36
Beard, Charles A., 20, 22, 25, 30–31, 44, 53–54, 66, 122. Works: *Economic Interpretation of the Constitution,* 34–36, 47–79, 70–73, 86, 105–106, 108; *Economic Origins of Jeffersonian Democracy,* 36–37, *Rise of American Civilization,* 41–42; "Written History as an Act of Faith," 21–22, 28–30
Beard, Mary, 41
Becker, Carl, 20, 25, 26–31, 33, 118; "Everyman His Own Historian," 21, 26–28
Bellesiles, Michael, 162–164
Belz, Herman, 158
Berthoff, Roland, 133
Bible, the, 168, 172, 175
Biddle, Nicholas, 17, 37–38, 77, 97
Billington, Ray Allen, 17
Bill of Rights, 107, 152, 178
Binkley, Winfred, 75
Biography, 11, 14–15, 64, 78, 109, 144–147, 153
Bisson, Tom, 111
Black history, 117–119, 133n., 157
Blacks, 42, 104–105, 109–111, 113–114, 133, 142
Blackstone, Sir William, 136, 172, 181
Blowup (movie), 6
Bogue, Allan, 99

Bolingbroke, first viscount, 173, 174–175
Bonner, Thomas, 77
Boorstin, Daniel, 82, 88, 144
Borah, William E., 43
Boston Globe, 163
Boyle, Gerry, 93
Bridenbaugh, Carl, 111–112, 128
Brooklyn College, 92, 117
Brown, Robert E., 68, 70, 78, 105–106
Browns of Providence, R.I., 61
Brown University, 60, 85–86, 90–93, 109–112
Brown v. *Board of Education,* 104
Bryan, Mary, 57
Bryan, William Jennings, 42
Bumstead, Jack, 112
Burlamaqui, Jean Jacques, 153–172
Burnett, Edmund Cody, 132
Burney, Fanny, 16
Business History Review, 99
Butler, Pierce, 185

Caesar, Julius, 2
Cain, James M., 51
Calhoun, John C., 39, 156
Calvin, John, and Calvinism, 23, 32, 120
Capitalism, 32, 40–41, 99–100, 106, 120–123, 146–147, 158–159
Capital Times (Madison), 70, 83
Carnegie, Andrew, 42
Celtic thesis, 127–135
Character, concept of, 16, 179–180. *See also* Ambition; Avarice; Civic humanism

Charleston Library Society, 57
Cheney, Lynne, 151, 157
Chesterfield, fourth earl of, 178
Chicago, 14–15, 24, 64, 77
Chicago Medical Society, 77
Cicero, 2, 172
Civic humanism, 146, 148,
    173–174, 182–183, 185
Civil War, 31, 41, 57, 102,
    104, 158
Claremont graduate school, 102
Clark, Thomas, 75
Clay, Henry, 38, 40
Cleveland, Grover, 42
Cliometrics, 119, 169–170
Coker, Ala., 139
Colbourn, Trevor, 102
Cold War, 122n., 158
Cole, Arthur H., 99
Coleman, Peter, 62
Columbia, S.C., 13, 58
Columbia University, 22, 74, 85,
    96–97, 105, 162, 164, 168
Commentary, 105, 153
Commerce, 13–14, 58–59,
    99–100, 170
Committee on Public Informa-
    tion, 24–26
Common law, 147, 169
Communism, 30, 46, 65
Community colleges, 115–116
Confederation period, 58, 61,
    70–71, 107–108
Congress, U.S., 23, 37, 38, 39,
    42, 44, 48
Congress of Racial Equality, 110
Connecticut, 13–14, 71, 73
Conservation, 99
Conservatives and conservatism,
    65–66, 123, 155

Constitution, U.S., 33–35,
    71, 72, 147–150, 167,
    184–186
Constitutional Convention,
    15–16, 71–73, 148, 167–
    168, 175
Coolidge, Calvin, 45
Cooper, Leon, 91
Cornell University, 75, 99
Corosso, Vincent, 99
Corporations, 42, 43, 45, 121,
    123–124, 173
Coxey's Army, 42
Craven, Avery, 41n.
Creel, George, 24–26
Crittenden, Christopher C., 58
Crowl, Philip A., 68
Crump, "Boss" E. H., 77
Curti, Merle, 55, 65, 87–88
Curtin, Philip, 118

Daily Texan, 53
Debts, private, 9, 12, 35, 37,
    68, 72
Debts, public, 12–13, 34–35,
    38, 59, 68–69, 70–73
Decker, Leslie E., 80, 99, 109,
    125–126
Declaration of Independence,
    174, 175–176, 180–181
Deism, 177
Delaware, 61, 69, 71
Democracy, 40, 97–98, 120
Democratic Party, 42, 44, 159
Descartes, René, 3
Detroit, 89, 111, 113
Detroit Edison Company, 80
Dickens, Charles, 16
Dickinson, John, 148
Diderot, Denis, 172

Dishonesty among historians,
  11, 22, 25–26, 30, 82,
  83–85, 114, 142, 160–164.
  See also Plagiarism
Dodd, William E., 25
Dowling, Dick, 49
Draper, Lyman C., 18
Dred Scott, 77
DuBois, W. E. B., 117
Duke University, 13, 117
Dunning, William E., 117
Durrell, Lawrence, 6–8

Easterby, J. Harold, 58
Economic interpretation of his-
  tory, 21, 31–46, 54, 73–74,
  86–87, 98, 105–106, 108
Edison, Thomas, 93, 157
Elections, 36, 38, 42, 43, 44, 45,
  103, 110
Electric utilities, 45, 63, 66, 70,
  79–80, 93
Ellis, Joseph, 160
Emory University, 103–104,
  162, 163
Engerman, Stanley L., 119, 141
Enlightenment, French, 171–172
Era of Good Feelings, 37

Fame, concept of, 108, 147,
  177, 180. *See also* Character,
  concept of
Farmer, James, 110
Farmers, 13, 32–34, 37–38,
  41–42, 71, 98, 103, 119, 128
Farrell, James T., 51–64
Federalism, 185
Federalist essays, 170–171
Federalists, 33, 36–37, 68–69,
  70–71

Fehrenbacher, Don, 77
Ferrell, Robert, 78
Fischer, David Hackett, 140–141
Fisk, Jim, 42
Fisk University, 117
Fogel, Robert W., 119, 141
Folsom, Burton W., 158
Football, 50, 53, 88–89
Ford, Guy Stanton, 25
Foreign relations, 43–45,
  120–122
Fox-Genovese, Elizabeth, 144
Franchise, 33, 35, 38, 42, 45,
  100–101, 113
Franklin, Benjamin, 173, 179
Franklin, John Hope, 117
Freedmen's Bureaus, 118
Freyer, Tony, 144
Frontier, the American, 17, 20,
  32, 38, 41, 97, 99, 121,
  127–130

Gardner, Lloyd C., 141
Gates, Paul Wallace, 75, 99
General Electric, 93
Genovese, Eugene, ix, 118–119
Georgia, 71, 100, 103, 131
Georgia Department of Archives
  and History, 57
Georgia Historical Society, 57
Georgia Tech, 104
German Americans, 24
Germany, 4, 25, 30
Gibbon, Edward, 3–4
G.I. Bill of Rights, 53
Ginger, Ray, 62
Goldwater, Barry, 110
Goodwin, Doris Kearns, 161
Gorham, Nathaniel, 73, 175
Gould, Jay, 42

Govan, Thomas P., 17, 77, 81, 97–98, 104, 126, 145–146
Grade inflation, 116
Granger Movement, 42
Grant, Ulysses S., 42, 45, 159
Gray, Lewis C., 127
Grayson, William, 168
Great Britain, 9, 25–26, 128–129, 139, 168–169
Great Depression, 45–46, 48, 84, 105, 122, 126
Greece, ancient, 2–3, 172
Greenback Movement, 42
Greens, Evarts B., 25
Grotius, Hugo, 153
Guggenheim Fellowship, 96

Hamilton, Alexander, 16, 36, 137, 144–147, 152, 171, 173, 180
Hammond, Bray, 97–98
Hancock, John, 168
Handlin, Mary, 100
Handlin, Oscar, 100, 140–143
Harding, Warren G., 35, 45
Hartz, Louis, 100
Harvard, 55, 117
Harvard Business School, 85, 98–99
Head, John, 112
Heath, Milton S., 100
Heather, Justin, 163
Hebrew Union College, 109
Hedges, James B., 60–61, 85–86, 91, 92, 111
Henry, Patrick, 168
Herding, 128–135
Herodotus, 2
Hesseltine, William B., 70, 84
Hexter, J. H., 5

Hichborn, Benjamin, 181
Hicks, John D., 42
Hidy, Ralph, 85, 99
Hilliard, Sam B., 118
Historical literacy, 155–160, 172–173
Historical records, 2, 18–19, 27, 47–79, 114, 163–164; doing research in, 8, 11–13, 56–62, 127. *See also* Library of Congress; National Archives; *and other specific repositories*
Historical Society, The, 164
History, definitions of, 1–11, 27–28, 95
History Today, 133
Hodder, F. W., 31
Hofstadter, Richard, 40, 105–107
Holst, Hermann von, 74
Holt, Michael F., 156
Hoover, Herbert, 45
Hughes, Charles Evans, 43
Humble Oil company, 49
Hume, David, 4, 102, 173–174
Hunter, Louis C., 80
Hutchinson, Anne, 32
Huthmacher, Joseph, 107

Ideology, 26, 102, 148, 184
Immigration, 42, 106–107, 123, 131–134
Imperialism, 43–44, 120–122
Indians, 40, 114, 118n., 123, 142, 157
Insull, Gladys Wallis, 15
Insull, Samuel, 14–15, 64, 78, 93–94
Insull, Samuel, Jr., 15, 78, 82–84

Intellectual history, 32–33, 101, 147–149

Isidore of Seville, 3

Jackson, Andrew, 38–40, 173; age of, 31, 101; Jacksonian democracy, 38, 40, 97–98, 156

Jackson State University, 114

Jameson, J. Franklin, 18, 25, 33

Jamieson, Perry D., 134

Jay, John, 168, 171

Jefferson, Thomas, 2, 136–139, 160, 168, 173, 179–180

Jeffersonian democracy, 32, 36–37, 38, 42, 98, 103, 137–139, 147

Jefferson Lecture, Sixteenth (NEH), 150. *See* Appendix

Jim Crow statutes, 104–105

Johnson, Hiram, 43

Johnson, Lyndon Baines, 110, 123, 161

Johnson, Samuel, 4, 171

Jones, Howard, 144

Jones, William, 37

Jordan, Winthrop, 118

Josephson, Matthew, 42

Journal of American History, 80, 162

Journal of Southern History, 75, 88, 131

Juries, 77, 169

Kansas, 30, 32, 78

Keeney, Barnaby, 85–86, 111

Kent State University, 114

Knopf, Alfred A., 81

Kohl, Lawrence Frederick, ix, 101n.

Kolko, Gabriel, 122–123, 141

Labor unions, 123, 136

Ladd, Everett C., 159–160

La Follette, Robert M., 43, 45

Land, Aubrey, 136

Lands, public, 42, 61, 73, 74, 100, 130

Larson, Henrietta, 99

Lasch, Christopher, 141

Latin, 168, 170, 182

Layne, Bobby, 88–89

League of Nations, 45

Lee, Harper, 133n.

Lee, Richard Henry, 168, 178

Lee, Robert E., 159

Lewis, Archie, 79

Leyburn, James G., 131

Libby, Orin G., 33–34, 35, 36

Liberals and liberalism, 40, 65–66, 91, 119–120, 125, 151, 155, 159–160

Library Company (Philadelphia), 171

Library of Congress, 18, 49, 59

Lincoln, Abraham, 126, 159

Lindgren, James, 162–163

Lipset, Seymour Martin, 159–160

Literacy, 116, 169–170, 175

Livy, 2

Locke, John, 120, 174, 181

Logan, Frenise, 104

Long, Huey, 77

Lord, Clifford, 62–63, 66, 70, 74–75, 78, 79–85

Lord, Sterling, 108–109

Lowden, Frank O., 43

Loyalists, 33, 184

Lukacs, John, 144

Lund, P. R., 52

Lytle, Andrew, 132n.

Macdonald, H. Malcolm, 53
Madison (Wis.), 65–66, 70
Madison, James, 102, 145, 171, 172
Maier, Pauline, 144
Malcolm, Joyce, 163
Malin, James C., 30–31, 77
Manchester, Harland, 60, 79
Manchester, Laetitia, 79
Marcy, K. L., 53
Marion (Ohio) *Star,* 35
Marshall, John, 168
Maryland, 68, 71, 131
Maryland Hall of Records, 59, 68
Massachusetts, 34, 71, 72, 73, 100, 107, 181
Mather, Cotton, 32
Maysville Road veto, 39
McAvoy, Howie, 52
McCaleb, Walter F., 74
McCarthyism, 66, 106, 157
McCormick, Richard P., 61, 69, 100–101
McDonald, Ellen Shapiro, 13, 16, 97, 128, 132, 144–145, 164, 165n.
McDonald, Forrest: at American History Research Center, 74–77, 78, 79–85; and the Bicentennial, 147–152; at Brown, 85–86, 90–96, 109–112; childhood, 49–50; education, 16, 20, 49–51, 53–55, 74, 78, 136; family, 53, 56, 58, 60, 95–97; fellowships, 54–55, 56, 96, 136; motivation, viii–ix, 11–12, 17, 18–19, 165–166; in the navy, 51–52; politics of, 65–66, 110, 151, 158; as researcher, 12–14, 51–52, 54,

55–62, 86–88, 132, 144, 153; in Spain, 97, 128; at State Historical Society of Wisconsin, 62–63, 69–70; at University of Alabama, 139, 143–144, 165n; visiting professorships, 13, 96, 150; at Wayne State University, 110, 114–116, 128, 136; in West Florida, 136–137; as writer, 17, 51, 70, 74, 96, 145, 152, 156. Books by: *Alexander Hamilton,* 144–147; *American Presidency,* 153, 155–156; *Constitutional History of the United States,* 144; *E Pluribus Unum,* 107–109, 147; *Insull,* 14, 93–95; *Last Best Hope,* 115–126; *Let There Be Light,* 79–81; *Novus Ordo Seclorum,* 147–149; *The Phaeton Ride,* 136; *The Presidency of George Washington,* 137; *The Presidency of Thomas Jefferson,* 37n., 137–139; *Requiem,* 152, 167n.; *States' Rights and the Union,* 31n., 156; *The Torch is Passed,* 109; *We the People,* 66, 70–74, 78, 79, 81–85, 86–88
McDonald, William Edward (Jim), 53
McIlwain, C. H., 30
McLaughlin, Andrew C., 23, 25
McLoughlin, William G., 91, 111–112
McNeil, Donald, 85
McWhiney, Grady, 127–135, 138, 139

Meat Inspection Act, 43
Memphis, 77
Mercantilism, 120–121
Miller, Perry, 101
Miller, Raymond C., 79–80
Miller, William D., 77
Mississippi, 109–110
Mississippi Valley Historical Review, 80, 83
Monroe, James, 168
Montesquieu, baron de, 172, 183, 185–186
Mood, Fulmer: as historian, 17, 55, 64–65; and the profession, 37, 55, 60, 62; as teacher, 55–56, 59–60, 66, 79, 87, 145
Morgan, Edmund, 82, 144, 162
Morgan, J. P., 109
Morison, Samuel Eliot, 31, 65, 101
Morris, Gouverneur, 152
Morris, Richard B., 147
Morris, Robert, 73–74, 175
Mount Holyoke College, 160
Munro, Dana C., 25
Munroe, John A., 61, 69

Nash, Gary B., 157–158
National Archives, 48, 54, 59
National Endowment for the Humanities, 150–151, 157
Natural law, 153, 172
Natural rights, 180–181
Naval Officer Returns, 59
Navy, U.S., 37, 43, 103
Nevins, Allan, 57–58, 60
New Deal, 40, 42, 45–46, 97, 106, 122
New Hampshire, 71

New Hampshire State Library, 12
New History, 21, 26–29, 31, 33–46, 73, 98
New Jersey, 13, 61, 69, 71, 100–101
New Left, 78, 120–125
Newspapers, 24, 48, 53, 57, 170–171. *See also specific newspapers*
Newsweek, 133
Newton, Sir Isaac, 3
New York (city), 60, 105, 107, 170
New York (state), 13, 33, 72, 73
New York Review of Books, 162
New York Times, 50–51, 87, 88, 94, 107, 151, 161
Nichols, Roy Franklin, 61, 75
Niles, Nathaniel, 183
Nixon, Richard, 155, 161
Norris, George W., 43
North, the, 40, 41, 103, 119, 135
North Carolina, 68, 71, 72, 104, 131
Northwestern University, 162
Nullification, 39–40
Nye Committee, 44

O'Neill, Thomas P., "Tip," 75
Open Door policy, 121
Orange (Texas), 49, 56
Organization of American Historians, 157
Owsley, Frank, 127

Panama Canal, 44
Panic of 1819, 37; Panic of 1907, 44
Paper-money movement, 12–13, 72

Parrington, Vernon L., 32
Patterson, Caleb Perry, 74
Paxson, Frederick L., 25
Pembroke College, 92–93, 165n.
Pendleton, Edmund, 168
Pennsylvania, 13, 71, 72, 73, 100
Pessen, Edward, 101
Philadelphia, 37, 71, 131, 170
Philadelphia Society, 132n., 154
Philosophes, 26, 172
Plagiarism, 64–65, 142,
  161–162
Plato, 172–173
Plutarch, 2, 172, 180
Pocock, J. G. A., 102
Political economy, 173–174
Political parties, 35–37, 38, 42,
  44, 45, 100–101, 159–160
Political philosophy, 53–54,
  147–148, 170–171, 174, 185
Pollock, Norman, 107, 141
Polybius, 2, 172
Pool, William Clay, 58
Pope, Alexander, 171
Popular Science, 64
Populist Movement, 42, 103,
  106–107, 173
Potter, David M., 86–104
Pratt, Julius, 43
Presidency, 137–139, 153–156
Primm, James S., 100
Progressive Era, 31, 35, 43–45,
  70, 106–107
Providence, R.I., 61, 163
Propaganda, 22–26, 159
Public virtue, 182
Publish or perish, 18
Pulitzer Prize, 32, 75, 77, 97
Pure Food and Drug Act, 43
Puritans, 32

Quasi-War with France, 36

Raborn, George W. (Tater), 50
Radical Republicans, 118
Radicals and radicalism, 65–66,
  91, 105–106, 113–114,
  120–125, 141–142, 157–159
Radio, 24, 50
Railroads, 32, 42, 61, 99
Rainey, Glenn, 104
Rakove, Jack, 163
Randall, James G., 41
Ranke, Leopold von, 4, 6, 22,
  29, 31
Ratification of the Constitution,
  33–34, 35, 68–69, 70–73
Reagan, Ronald, 150, 155
Reconstruction, 31, 41,
  102–103, 117–118
Records of the Loan of 1790,
  47–48, 59, 71–72
Redlich, Fritz, 99
Religion, 3–4, 9–10, 65, 101,
  119, 120–121, 169, 177–178
Republicanism, 147, 181–183
Republican Party, 44, 159–160
Revolution, American, 9, 26,
  33, 124, 159, 180
Revolutionary War debts,
  47–48, 59, 70–73
Rhode Island, 13, 72
Rittenhouse, David, 168
Robber barons, 42, 99, 103
Robbins, Caroline, 102
Robinson, James Harvey, 22
Rockefeller, John D., 42
Rome, ancient, 2–3, 171, 172
Roosevelt, Franklin, 40, 45–46,
  94, 120, 122
Roosevelt, Theodore, 43–44

Roosevelt Corollary to the Monroe Doctrine, 44, 120
Rothstein, Morton, 99–100
Rousseau, Jean-Jacques, 172
Rush, Benjamin, 168, 172
Rutgers, 100

San Francisco, 163
Saturday Review, 86
Scarborough, Lem, 56
Schiff, Jacob, 109
Schlesinger, Arthur, 33
Schlesinger, Arthur, Jr., 40, 97
Schuyler, Robert Livingston, 88
Scientific history, viii, 4, 21
Scotch-Irish, 131–135
Scotland, 134
Second Amendment, 162
Sectionalism, 127–135
Segregation, 103–105
Shay's Rebellion, 34
Sherman, Richard, 107
Sherman, Roger, 175
Shugg, Roger, 82, 86, 94
Shyrock, Richard H., 75
Silver Spring, Md., 58–59
Sinclair, Upton, 43
Singer, Charles, 58
Simons, Algie, 34
Slavery, 13–14, 32, 116–119, 137
Smiles, Samuel, 14
Smith, Adam, 173–174
Smith, Goldwin, 128–129
Smith, Page, 122, 123–125
Smith, T. C., 30
Social history, 129–135
Social Science Research Council, 54–55, 61, 100
South, the, 36, 41, 42, 102–105, 118, 127–135

South Carolina, 39, 57, 71, 73, 104, 131, 185
South Carolina Department of Archives, 13–14, 58
Southern Living, 133
Spanish-American War, 43, 120
Sparks, Jared, 18
Stampp, Kenneth, 117–118
Stanford University, 159–160
State Councils of Defense, 23–24
State Historical Society of Wisconsin, 18, 62–63, 69, 80, 83–85
States' Rights, 39–40, 100, 156
Stephen, Kevin Forrest, 53
Stephens, H. Morse, 23
Stephenson, Wendell, 75
Sternstein, Jerome, 92
Steuart, Sir James, 173
Stilwell, Abner J., 84
Stourzh, Gerald, 102
Students, quality of, 92–93, 113–116, 143, 151, 156–157, 170
Subjectivism-relativism-presentism, viii, 21–23, 26–31, 104–105
Supreme Court, 35, 39, 167
Sweet, William Warren, 65

Tacitus, 2, 172
Taft, William Howard, 35, 44
Tansill, Charles, 122
Tariffs, 37, 38–39, 42, 100
Taylor, John, 168
Teaching, 17, 20–21, 49, 56, 74, 91, 141–142, 170. *See also* Community colleges; Grade inflation, Publish or perish;

Students, quality of; Tenure;
  Textbooks
Templeton, Kenneth, 85n.
Tenure, 62, 86, 111
Texas, 20, 49–50
Texas A&M, 66
Textbooks, 21, 26, 36, 42, 45,
  94, 109, 125–126
Thomas, Isaiah, 171
Thomas, Robert E., 69
Thucydides, 2
Tougaloo College, 109–110
Trade, 13, 33–34, 58, 59, 100,
  170, 183
Treaty of Versailles, 44
Tubman, Harriet, 159
Tuner, Frederick Jackson, 17,
  20–21, 25, 38–39; "The
  Significance of the Frontier
  in American History,"
  129–130; as teacher, 22, 33,
  34, 40, 55, 60

United States Naval Academy,
  161
University of Alabama, 138,
  139, 143
University of Buffalo, 105
University of Chicago, 74, 117
University of Chicago Press, 82,
  86, 93
University of Georgia, 136
University of Kansas, 30, 77
University of Kentucky, 75
University of Minnesota Press, 69
University of North Dakota, 36
University of Pennsylvania, 61
University of Texas, 20, 50, 56,
  65, 79, 88
University of Washington, 32

University of Wisconsin, 55, 70
University of Wisconsin Press, 69
University Press of Kansas, 137,
  139, 153, 155

VanDeMark, Brian, 161
Vanderbilt, Cornelius, 42
Vermont, 163
VerSteeg, Clarence, 144
Vattel, Emmerich de, 153, 172
Vietnam war, 113, 124, 160
Virginia, 9, 33, 59, 69, 72, 104,
  131, 168
Virginia Bill of Rights, 177–178
Virginia Historical Society, 59
Virginia State Library, 59
Voltaire, 4, 172

Wade, Richard C., 104
Walpole, Sir Robert, 139
Washburn, Wilcomb, 158, 159
Washington, Bushrod, 168
Washington, George, 157, 175;
  character of, 15–16, 151,
  178, 180; in Constitutional
  Convention, 15, 152, 168; as
  general, 165; inaugural ad-
  dress, 186; as president, 137
Watson, Tom, 103, 107
Wayne State University,
  114–116, 128, 136
Webb, Walter Prescott, 20, 54, 56
Webster, Daniel, 38, 157
Webster, Noah, 168
Wentworth, John, 77
West Indies, 13, 58
West Point, 151
Weyerhaeuser company, 99
Whig interpretation of history,
  173

Wiebe, Robert, 144
William and Mary, College of,
102, 150
William and Mary Quarterly,
102, 132, 144, 163
Williams, Roger, 32
Williams, T. Harry, 77
Williams, William Appleman,
78, 120–122, 141, 158
Williamson, Chilton, 101
Williamson, Joel, 104
Wilson, Woodrow, 23, 25,
44–45, 120
Wisconsin, 18, 43, 62, 65–66,
69, 81
Wisconsin Magazine of History,
80, 82
Wisconsin Utilities Association,
63, 78, 80, 81
Wodehouse, P. G., 16

Women, 45, 114, 123, 142,
157, 158
Wood, Gordon, 102
Woodward, C. Vann, 87,
102–105
Worcester, Mass., 171
Works Progress Administration,
48
World War I, 22–26, 44–45,
110, 122
World War II, 48, 158
Worthington, Harvey, 78
Wright, Esmond, 107–108
Wriston, Henry Merritt, 91
Writing, 17–19, 69–71, 74, 94–95,
125–126, 145–146, 152, 156
Wynes, Charles, 104

Yale University, 86
Younger, Richard, 77